KATHY CARR
MISSION TO THE
UMATILLA

REVIEW AND HERALD PUBLISHING ASSOCIATION
Washington, D.C. 20012

Copyright © 1981 by the
Review and Herald Publishing Association

Editor: Thomas A. Davis
Design: Alan Forquer
Cover: Jack Purdue

Library of Congress Cataloging in Publication Data

Carr, Kathy, 1926-
   Mission to the Umatilla.

   1. Umatilla Indians—Missions.   2. Seventh-day Adventists—
Missions—Oregon.   3. Missions—Oregon.   I. Title.
E99.U4C4   266'.67795   81-11997
ISBN 0-8280-0107-3   AACR2

Printed in U.S.A.

CONTENTS

THE TRAGEDY OF MARA

VERNA SAT UP with a start. What was that noise? Was it the doorbell? No. Her husband, Lee, had been shaking her gently. "Verna, Verna, wake up!" She began scrambling out of bed in the dark, feeling for her slippers and the light switch.

As she flipped on the light Lee whispered, "Verna, the police are here!" That shocked her fully awake. A glance at her watch showed her that it was five o'clock in the morning. As she put on her robe and hurried after Lee toward the front room, she thought, Could they be bringing Mara home?

Sometimes Verna regretted having become a foster mother. Why did so many crises have to happen on Friday night? She had spent most of the night calling and searching for Mara. Now she felt confused and dizzy from lack of sleep.

She hurried to the door, expecting to see a penitent or defiant foster daughter. Instead, she saw a large policeman, all alone.

"Oh," stammered Verna. "I thought it might be

Mara. Have you found her?"

"Good morning," he said. "I'm Trooper Jackson, of the Oregon State Police. Are you Mrs. Lee Clay?"

"Yes, sir," Verna replied. "Please come in."

"And you are the foster mother of Mara Thomas?" he continued as he stepped inside the door and glanced quickly about the room.

"Yes, I have had her for a week. Mara is a ward of the court."

"Mrs. Clay, we may have found Mara, but I'm afraid I have bad news for you," said the officer.

Verna's hand rose slightly in a protective gesture. "Oh, what is it? Is Mara in jail? We think someone gave her liquor."

"No, Mrs. Clay, she's not in jail." Officer Jackson shook his head. "We believe your foster daughter has been struck by a car. She has been taken to the emergency unit of St. Mary's Hospital in Walla Walla. Would you please come to the hospital and identify her for us?"

Lee Clay looked down at his slippered feet. "Do you want me to go with you?"

"No, dear," said Verna, glancing at her husband. "I can go alone."

But the officer shook his head. "No," he said firmly. "Do not go alone, Mrs. Clay. You go with her, sir."

Lee nodded in understanding. "I'll get dressed at once."

Verna realized then that seeing Mara might be a bad shock. She must be seriously hurt. What had happened to their beautiful foster daughter who had run away into the night? Mara, with the shining dark hair and big, flashing brown eyes. "Oh, Mara," whispered Verna. She turned toward Officer Jackson as he started out the door. "We'll come as quickly as possible," she assured him.

"Will you be there?"

"No, I have another matter to attend to, but another officer will be at the hospital waiting for you. If this is indeed Mara you will want to cancel the runaway report you placed with our office." The policeman nodded and was gone.

Returning to her bedroom, Verna impulsively glanced into Mara's room. The bed was smoothly made and untouched. Verna's thoughts raced as she hesitated by the door. What might Mara need at the hospital? Across the bed was spread the beautiful new long dress that Mara had planned to wear to her first Sabbath church service. It was a pretty red and white. Mara looked so radiant in it, with her long dark hair and beautiful eyes. She was so eager to wear the dress that she kept it out where she could see it.

Mara had owned few pretty dresses in her lifetime. When she arrived at the Clays' home only a week before on a Friday evening, she had brought nothing but an extra pair or two of ragged jeans and a few tops. The social worker promised to provide an emergency clothing order early the following week.

That first weekend Mara was too ashamed to attend church in her shabby clothing, so Verna stayed home with her, and they became acquainted. Mara was 16, Indian, and presented a placement problem for the Children's Services Department. She was a court ward and an alcoholic, with a behavior disorder and a history of multiple runaways.

Mara's parents had parted long before, after a drunken brawl. Her father's new wife also drank with him, and she allowed Mara to drink. Sometimes drugs were available to her.

One day Mara's own mother overdosed on a particularly lethal drug and blew her mind. This made Mara very sad, for now her mother was a "vegetable," unaware of her whereabouts, unable to recognize even her own children. Mara explained to Verna that her mother would spend the rest of her life simply breathing in and out, being put into a bed at night, and being dressed, fed, and lifted into a wheelchair by day. Mother's worries were over for life, for she would never get any better, according to the doctors.

"My father is gone too," continued Mara. "I loved him so much. But he and my stepmother fought and drank all the time. Then one day my father drowned while fishing from a boat. My life has been pretty mixed up, I guess," she added apologetically.

"Sometimes I get to wondering what will happen to me, and my head boils inside. I get angry and want to scream. Drinking makes me feel better, and drugs help me to forget. I don't want to end up like my mother, just sitting and staring and not knowing even her own relatives. But now I've drunk so much that I can't quit. I know I'll die if I don't quit. Sometimes I think I'd rather die so I could be with my father."

Mara put her hands to her head. "Oh, I don't know what I want, do I?" She looked appealingly at Verna.

"Mara, even though God can't bring back your mother and father, He loves you just as you are. He understands all your problems. He loves you so much that He let His only Son come to this world to die for your sins. Trust Him. Ask Him to help you. He'll hear you and change your life so that you will be happy again," Verna said earnestly.

"Maybe so," murmured Mara doubtfully. She hadn't had much contact with God. His name was more familiar as a swear word than as a prayer word. But she looked interested and thoughtful, as if she might like to hear more about God someday.

On Sunday, Mara's aunt, grandmother, and uncles from the nearby Umatilla Reservation came to see her and took her on a picnic. They were really friendly to Verna and her husband, much to Verna's surprise, for Indian relatives often don't like their children to be placed with white foster parents. They had a good visit with Verna and her husband after the picnic.

Mara was exceptionally well-behaved during the rest of the week. She had a weekday job at a local day-care center, and was gone most of the time. She loved her work, caring for the small children, and they loved her. She was gentle with them and responded well to their needs.

On Wednesday afternoon, after Verna picked up the clothing order, they had gone shopping together. In addition to basic clothing there was enough money to purchase pants, tops, a jacket, and one dress. Mara had loved the red-and-white frock at first sight.

Social workers refer to the initial phase of foster placement as the "honeymoon period." During this phase the foster child is usually well-behaved, compliant, and cooperative. Wise foster mothers soon learn to watch for children who are exceptionally well-behaved, because they know that within a few days or weeks an equal and opposite reaction may set in, suddenly, violently, and without warning. Destructive behavior, defiance of rules, running away, drinking, and drug use usually follow. During this second phase teen placements falter and often fail. Only a strong, understanding, experienced foster parent can exercise gentle control and handle the shock of listening to a once sweet foster child explode, perhaps, into a raging, drunken demon, lashing out in hostility toward those who want to help him, and screaming a stream of filthy, abusive language. Many foster parents simply call the caseworker during the peak of the crisis and demand immediate removal, not caring or understanding that this phase, too, will pass.

The honeymoon period for Mara lasted just a week. On Friday afternoon Verna, who ran a small candle-and-gift shop next door to her home, suggested to Mara that she might like to go bike riding. Verna kept a well-worn bicycle that the police had once brought to her for foster children that she kept. Mara enjoyed the ride. Later she took her small beaded purse from the bedroom and walked to the crossroads store across the street. From there she vanished.

When Mara did not return by closing time, Verna locked the shop and searched for the girl. Failing to find her, she went to the police station to file a runaway report with a description of Mara. She also called the girl's social worker, who told her not to hunt or worry. Mara's usual runaway pattern was to head for California.

But now—Verna hated to think what might happen now.

It was dawn when the Clays arrived at St. Mary's Hospital. They quickly found the intensive care unit and reported to the nurses' station. An officer was waiting for them there. Quietly they entered the small room. It had to be Mara. It was Mara. But oh, how changed! She was unconscious and moaning. Her face was swollen and unrecognizable: her abdomen was distended. Clearly she was fatally injured. Verna, aghast at the dreadful sight, identified the girl by her clothing and beaded purse, then tiptoed out. She was glad now that she had not come alone. She clung to Lee's hand.

The officer explained that Mara had been found hitchhiking several miles away, near Milton-Freewater, and had been stopped by police, who had her description. She was intoxicated and insisted that she was eighteen. Suddenly a car came around the bend toward them. Mara stepped out, apparently intending to flag it down and escape. Just as she stepped out, the car struck her. The officer was unable to give the Clays the name of the driver.

Verna left the hospital, promising to return as soon as she could. She must notify relatives and the Indian agency and cancel the runaway report. Before she completed attending to these matters, word came from the hospital that Mara had died.

Sadly, the Grandmother and aunts received Mara's belongings, including the new dress that had never been worn. The grandmother thanked Verna for being so kind to Mara. Later Verna took a cake and casserole dish to the relatives.

Instead of the customary beaded buckskin tunic, Mara was buried in the new long dress, as a favor to her foster mother. The funeral was held in the Presbyterian church at Tutuilla, on the south reservation. Verna attended. From the time she arrived until the end of the service she was never left alone. Mara's grandmother assigned a young male relative to guide her through the service.

Everyone stood around outside the church until the hearse arrived. It backed up to about six feet from the steps. A Nez Perce Indian minister from Idaho read part of the service as he faced the casket. Later the casket was taken into the church foyer, and the service continued inside the church. Part of the service was in English and part in the tribal language. The congregation sang several songs in their language. Then everyone filed out. On the closed casket was a big beautiful photograph of Mara. Upon seeing the picture, Verna lost her composure. She knew that Indians are not supposed to display emotion at funerals. Helplessly Verna let the tears flow.

Funerals always made her cry. She hoped they would forgive her weakness.

Soon several young girls dressed in Mara's clothing, as is the custom, filed out, took some of the flowers, and stood close by the casket when it was brought out. It was not a gloomy ceremony. Mara's sisters, who were being raised by another grandmother, were there. Her mother sat in her wheelchair nearby, unaware of what was happening and staring vacantly.

No one left until the grave was completely filled. Young men of the tribe took turns at the spade work, two at a time.

Much food had been prepared and placed in the church hall for a feast, as a symbol that life must go on. Verna was asked to stay for the meal. But she was too upset to eat, and declined, which was a mistake. Not eating with the Indians when asked was a dishonor to the deceased as well as to the survivors, but she did not yet know the custom. Later, when she learned the significance of what she had done, she apologized to Mara's grandmother and was forgiven her breach of etiquette. Since then, the two have become the best of friends. The grandmother often tells Verna's foster children to obey her and treat her well because of her kindness to Mara.

Because of Mara, Verna now vowed to spend her life working for the Indians. But how? Being a foster mother was not the total answer. Busy as she was with the shop and family, she could not crowd the desperate needs of the Indian children out of her mind. She and Lee prayed often for guidance.

One day she drove to the reservation to visit Mara's alcohol-and-drug counselor, to tell him that she wanted to do something for the Indian children before they became like Mara. She asked to start a Story Hour.

The counselor listened tolerantly, then shook his long

black braids and said, "Oh, you are emotional over Mara. You're like all the whites. You will come once and not come anymore."

Another counselor who was listening added, "We don't need any more religions in here fighting."

PEOPLE OF THE UMATILLA

MARA HAD BEEN a Umatilla Indian. For centuries her people had roamed, pitching their tepees by streams that rippled between the rolling Oregon hills. Bordering their land eastward were the Blue Mountains. On the west flowed the mighty Columbia River.

The men hunted wild game, which was abundant. The women dug roots in spring and picked and dried berries in summer. The tribe caught many salmon to be smoked and dried. Venison was dried in thin strips and stored in large, tightly-woven baskets. Roots, berries, and salmon were kept in the same kind of baskets. Summer was a busy time for the hunters and for the women, who worked at preserving food sufficient to last through the cold, harsh winters.

Among the Indians in the old days stories of Creation, the Flood, the confusion of languages, geological upheavals following the Flood, natural disasters, exploits of mighty men, and battles won or lost, customs, morals and manners, were all passed orally from generation to generation. Storytelling was one of the cultivated arts, a winter pastime to be pursued during cold, snowy days when children could not spend time playing outdoors.

There were two lodges for the children, one for boys and one for girls. The children sat around the central heating system, composed of many fire-heated rocks in the center of the lodge. Dressed warmly in buckskin clothing, ornamented with quills, hand-drilled beads, and occasionally shells obtained in barter from coastal tribes, they heard the stories of the early days of the world told by the old ones, the wise old grandmothers and white-haired tribal elders. They learned of herbs and bark and medicine from leaves. The children listened closely and learned well, for they knew that someday they must pass on these same stories and wisdom to their grandchildren in the honored tradition.

The Yakima, Nez Percé, Wallawalla, Cayuse, and Umatilla tribes were closely related. Each group was aware of its unique personality, strength, or weakness, as defined in tribal legends. The Nez Percé were noted for wisdom, bravery, and oratory. The Cayuse and Wallawallas were warriors and strong bowmen. The Yakimas and Umatillas were a kindly, peace-loving people.

In the early 1960s I was a social-service worker in Pendleton, with the Umatilla Reservation as my assigned area. During the few years that I worked among the Indians there I found the residents to be mostly a tribal mixture. When this area was made into a reservation in 1855, the Wallawalla and Cayuse tribes were moved to the traditional Umatilla camping grounds, the land of the blowing wind and the shifting sands. The word *Umatilla* means "water rippling over many stones." The original reservation comprised more than 300,000 acres of prairie, rolling hills, and timbered mountain. Now considerably less than one third of that property remains. Much of the tillable land has been sold or is leased by wheat ranchers.

Because the old tribal dances and ceremonies were summarily pronounced as heathen and forbidden by the whites, only a few customs remain. For many years the local government attempted to legislate its own form of civilization upon these children of nature, with amazing inconsistencies. Recognizing no boundaries, white settlers continued to pour into the area and to take what they would from the Indians, who were supposedly under the protection of the Government on their designated territory. Apparently anything considered heathen was to be destroyed, for ruthless white men rode rampant through the reservation, killing stock, stealing horses, destroying property, and even attacking the women and children.

Horrified at the pillage of their rights and property, the Indians retaliated in kind. Between 1868 and 1878, the several tribes of western Idaho and eastern Oregon, angry at the steady influx of white settlers at the expense of Indian freedoms and rights, decided they had had enough. Indians engaged whites in numerous small skirmishes in Umatilla and other eastern Oregon counties.

In the summer of 1878, after white settlers experienced a number of Indian raids, General O. O. Howard marched on the marauding Indians. A coalition of Bannocks, Snakes, and Paiutes met the troops in several indecisive battles. Finally in July, 1878, Chief Egan of the Bannocks led a large band of Snakes and Bannocks across the Blue Mountains westward toward the Umatilla Reservation. Egan and his warriors met and routed a group of white volunteers at Willow Springs in southern Umatilla County. Two days later, at Battle Mountain, General Howard drove the Indians back toward the Blue

Mountains, but not for long. Within the fastnesses of the mountains the Indians regrouped and surged out again. For several days the skirmishes continued. General Howard had met his match in Egan.

Strangely, a chief from the Umatilla Reservation, Umapine, a man who desired peace, volunteered to break the Indian resistance. Knowing that if Chief Egan could be killed, his followers would flee, this tall, powerfully built leader set out with a few followers toward the Bannock encampment. Ambushing and murdering the Bannock chief by night, Umapine added a few of Egan's close henchmen to the casualty list as well, and calmly showed up the next day at the Umatilla agency with a few grisly souvenirs to prove his conquest.

With their leader gone, the Bannock coalition shattered. General Howard routed the warriors, captured many of them, and sent the survivors to the nearby Yakima Reservation for temporary custody.

The tribes maintained an uneasy peace with the whites, who prevented any other uprising by simply hemming them in, confining them strictly to the designated small reservations, and settling the land confiscated from the Indians.

In only a few years the Indians witnessed the destruction of their whole way of life. They lost their freedom to roam about and live off the land, and watched helplessly as white men destroyed and polluted their revered earth-mother, with whom they had lived in harmony for so long. They also heard the words of the white man's religion. The words sounded good in their ears. But they watched while whiskey was given to their young men. They saw unfair dealings and mistreatment. They saw degradation and felt the pinch of want. Worst of all, they saw white men repeatedly break their word with the Indians.

The Indians not only saw the land polluted, they saw the food and the fur-game animals disappear. The salmon, beloved food staple—king salmon—no longer choked the waterways, forcing their way upstream into the shallows to spawn and die.

The Indians quickly became distrustful of a religion that could allow such things to happen. There is still little justice available to them, and they are the recipients of much discrimination.

I'm not suggesting that the Indians of the Northwest would have lived ideal lives had white men not invaded their land. They had many diseases that herbs could not help. Early explorers such as Lewis and Clark commented in their journals that they treated much sickness, stomach disorders, and eye problems, as well as disabling injuries, among the Indians. But we can learn from them in that they respected the land, learned to live within its limitations, and took from it only what they needed to live. And the land flourished under such a simple way of life.

Largely unseen and ignored for most of the year, the Umatilla Indians come into the spotlight at Pendleton Roundup time in mid-September. Then out come the heavily beaded, quilled and fringed buckskin tunics, the highly decorated moccasins, beaded headbands, the feathers, the long, trailing war bonnets (decorated mostly with chicken and turkey feathers, I was comforted to discover), and fringed, ornamented horse trappings. Whether or not they ride at any other time of year, Indians ride beautiful horses during roundup days, and they do so as if glued to their horses. Short hair is augmented with braided beaver strips and bound with beaded bands.

Tepees, usually relegated to rural back yards and used for smoking salmon, are hauled to the Roundup grounds, where the Indians erect an Indian village for the tourists to see. For a wild, wonderful week the Indians are paraded and pampered. Then they are expected to disappear again for another year, somewhat like Christmas ornaments.

Everyday dress for the older women is a long skirt and loose-fitting overblouse, both dark, a necklace or two of small beads, a dark scarf tied over the braided hair, and, on cool days, a square, fringed Pendleton blanket, made by the local woolen mill, for wearing around the shoulders. The adult men, who like Western attire, favor a tall, round-crowned broad-brimmed hat, usually trimmed with a beaded band, to wear over their braids. The younger men and women wear modern, casual jeans and shirts.

The younger Indians are literate and often well-educated; but very soon after I began working with the Indians I learned that I had to carry an inked stamp pad with me, as well as a box of Kleenex, so that the older members of the tribe could affix their thumbprint to legal documents, rather than write an "X." The women, especially, appreciated the Kleenex to wipe the ink off their thumbs after this messy procedure.

It was quite an occasion when one of the regal Indian ladies paid me a visit at the office, sweeping in, head up and proud, trailing her long, black, fringed shawl, followed by a servile interpreter who hovered about and made known the reason for the visit.

In the presence of these tribal princesses—and several of them were royal in their own right—one listened more than one spoke, and politeness was the order of the hour. I can recall how thrilled I was when one of them, becoming impatient with her clumsy interpreter, favored me with a few sentences of broken English. After that she came without an interpreter, and we got on just fine without a go-between.

Many of the old ones are gone now, and, sadly, the Nez Percé and Cayuse dialects are dying out, for the language of The People, as they call themselves, is flowing and musical.

Long ago many of the Indians took Christian names. But some of them retained for surnames that of a ranking member of their family. Thus, while you will meet the Burkes, Moores, Gordons, Van Pelts, McKays, Minthorns, and Williamses, you will also encounter such surnames as Showaway (from the Cayuse name Show-a-wa), Cowapoo, Shoeships, Kash Kash, Wak Wak, Willy Willy, Bearchum, Hoptowit, Wannasey, Bad Roads, Half Moon, Fat Elk, Jim, Joe, Bill, Sam, and Charley.

For a long time I was puzzled when one of the clients would call in to say, "Oh—ah—I'm using another name now. I'll be going by George now instead of Beaver, I guess."

"Oh, thanks for telling me. I'll make the necessary changes. Did you get married?"

"No."

"Did you get divorced from Sam?"

"No."

"Are you living with somebody else?"

"Well—ah—I'll be living with Jim George now, I guess."

"Oh," lamely.

What was going on? This musical chairs names business would happen every so often and in bunches. Months later I discovered that the old annual custom of wife trading was still secretly being practiced—by some. Well, sometimes when you can't respect the custom, you just have to listen, learn, and keep your mouth shut!

Deeply sensitive to seasonal changes in earth, water, and sky, Indians respond to beauty in nature. Many of them feel that their beliefs are just as good and not nearly so confusing as the many conflicting Christian faiths that clamor about them. Yet they are not happy. They want a better way of life. They drink to forget sorrow.

But they will respond only when they see faith evidenced in action over a long period of time. No amount of preaching has any effect.

This is why it is necesary for those who would show the Indians a better way of life to live among them, to learn to love them as they are, respect their culture and customs, and learn from them. And the would-be benefactors must mind their manners, be good neighbors, keep their word, refrain from gossip, and live before the Indians that better way of life. Only then will any impact be made upon the native Americans.

We cannot expect these native folk, who for the most part live quietly and unseen by us who adhere to the mad pace of the freeways and the workaday world, to think as we do, dress as we do, work as we do, or adhere to the same standards we do.

We whites are such conformists to our own way of life that we find it difficult to tolerate, or at least adjust to, anyone who appears different. But get this straight: The Indian will never think as you do. So let him walk in peace, thinking his own thoughts. If you have any contacts with him let him see what Jesus has done for you in your own daily walk and in your thoughts. He may in time decide to follow Jesus because he sees Jesus in you.

BEGINNINGS AND A DECISION

VERNA CLAY could never forget the Indian children she had kept in her home during her years as a foster mother. She had cared for many white children, too, but they had more going for them. Programs were set up for them that were not so readily available to Indian children. Surely she and Lee could do something for these spiritually needy Indian children.

Back from another futile trip to the reservation one day, Verna sat down behind the counter of her candle shop to reminisce and ponder what to do next. She thought back over the years that she and Lee had held Story Hours. Funny how she got started. Years ago, when her own children were small, they lived in Centralia, Washington. Verna discovered that a few of the neighborhood children delighted in coming to her house and listening to the stories she was telling to her children. Each day a few more children would show up, until she had quite a group.

Well, she had been wondering about a missionary project. This might be just right. And so it was. The neighbor children benefited as much as her own; and she received a great deal of practice in the art of storytelling.

Years later, when the Clays moved to Stateline, Oregon, they decided to continue this as a mission project. Several of the Stateline church members had considered beginning a branch Sabbath school in the small town of Weston, a few miles away, where there was no church, but a Story Hour seemed to be a more practical way to begin.

Verna smiled as she remembered the old deserted morgue she and Lee found to rent. They recruited a group of young adults from the Stateline church to help with the cleaning. It was dusty, dirty work. Even Verna's father, who was in his nineties, helped decorate. Soon it was clean and ready to use.

The children flocked in to that first Story Hour. And they kept coming back, week after week. Attendance was good. Forty or more children crowded into that old morgue.

Noticing the singular success of the program, another church group began holding special programs on the same afternoon as Story Hour. The number of children dwindled a bit, but they still kept coming.

One day in particular was still vivid in Verna's mind. Lee planned to take pictures of the Story Hour children. The opposing church group also scheduled a program for the same day. The children solved this dilemma neatly by attending the other church program first, then rushing breathlessly over to Story Hour. At the end of Story Hour they were all there to have their picture taken.

The Stateline church group distributed *Signs of the Times,* and tried to become acquainted with the residents of Weston. On one occasion a woman in Weston lost all her belongings in a fire. Hearing about the tragedy,

Verna began gathering quilts, blankets, and household goods. Next day she took all these items to the woman who was staying with friends. To Verna's surprise the pastor from the rival church was there. Upon being introduced, Verna dropped her bundle of bedding and shook his hand. The preacher said, "Mrs. Clay, I've heard about you."

Verna grinned mischievously at him and blurted, "Oh, was it good or bad?"

He replied, "Under that connotation, good."

Once the ice was broken, there was a bit less rivalry. But the Story Hour had fluctuations in attendance. One summer the lady to whom Verna had given the bedding allowed her daughter to attend the Seventh-day Adventist summer camp. The daughter was baptized without her mother's permission. The mother was so angry when she found out that she wouldn't let her daughter come near Adventists again. She told everybody all over town how her daughter had been coerced into baptism, and suddenly no more children were coming. That incident just about ended the program. But it didn't end the message. Now, years later, the woman's son is an active, dedicated member of the Adventist Church.

What a discouraging time! You try to tell others about Jesus, spend time, money, and energy for months on end, and then, because of somebody else's error, everything you worked for instantly goes down the drain.

Verna sighed. That was a bad one. But when things looked darkest, there was Pastor Estel Richardson, telling the discouraged Story Hour group that when Satan works the hardest it's because he's worried. "Trust God. Don't quit now," he kept telling them.

Strange how that worked out. Instead of failing, the work expanded to nearby areas. In spite of the difficulties and opposition the group of persons who had joined Clays in sponsoring the Weston Story Hour were soon distributing *Signs* not only in Weston but to towns and villages close by. They began to see how God was working through the difficulties to better display His providences. The work prospered and, with Pastor Richardson's guidance, the group eventually organized into a company. Each family was assigned a certain area in which to distribute *Signs*. And there were results.

Verna recalled the day she and Lee went to Helix, a small village nestled in the midst of wheat fields. They completed their *Signs* distribution early. Parking the car in front of a store to wait for the rest of the group, Verna glanced through the store window at an elderly woman who was standing just inside the store. The woman had snow-white hair and was wearing a lovely lavender sweater.

Impulsively Verna said, "Let's go give her a *Signs*."

How surprised they were to discover that she was not only willing to take the *Signs* but that she had been a Seventh-day Adventist forty years before! Because of an unfortunate incident involving a dishonest fellow church member, she left the church in disappointment, and had not been back since.

Lee and Verna continued to visit their new friend in Helix and to leave papers for her to read. Eventually, Verna recalled with pleasure, she consented to meet Pastor Richardson and to take Bible studies. One Sabbath she was baptized. She was so happy to come back into the church.

"The Lord can bring good out of most any situation," said Verna aloud, as her husband walked in the door. "I must remember that especially now."

"What are you saying? Do you know it's after closing time?" Lee asked, smiling.

"I'm thinking out loud," said Verna. "I was remembering how we nearly quit the Story Hour in Weston, how we decided not to quit but to extend the work to Helix, Athena, Adams, and the other villages."

"When things look darkest," said Lee, "we should cling tighter to the Lord's hand. If Story Hour hadn't faltered we might never have met all those wonderful people in the outlying towns. Truly all things do work together for good, if we're doing what the Lord wants. Let's get some supper," he added. "I'm hungry."

Over the evening meal they continued the discussion.

"Once we organized into a company there was no stopping us," Lee recalled, "although we had quite a time deciding on the location of the new church after we had outgrown company status."

"By then we had expanded our outreach programs into so many other areas that Athena was a natural choice," said Verna. "And now look how God has blessed the new Blue Mountain church—nearly 200 members from such small beginnings. We can praise Him for His providences."

"Do you recall the time one of the pastors actually suggested that it was too expensive to sponsor the *Signs* distribution and wanted us to stop the program because there appeared to be no results?"

"We had to explain that we were a missionary-oriented church and wanted to remain true to our convictions."

"Everyone encouraged him to think positively, and we continued right on."

"It was during the next year, wasn't it, that Julie Overstreet was baptized?" asked Verna.

"That's right," replied Lee. "It was as a direct result of reading *Signs of the Times*. What if we had stopped?"

Julie Overstreet and her husband had owned a tavern

in Weston for several years. They worked long hours, but their business provided a good living. They enjoyed their work and often took a social drink themselves. The tavern was a popular little stopping place, and the Overstreets had a lot of friends.

Along with many of the residents of Weston, the Overstreets received a *Signs* every month. At first Julie promptly threw the magazine away. But sometimes she was too busy to do that. Eventually she accumulated a few copies on her coffee table.

One morning, as she was dusting the table, she accidentally knocked a *Signs* to the floor. As it fell it opened, and she glanced at it to see an article explaining why God allows so much human suffering. She had been wondering about that for a long time. Intrigued, she sat down to read, and kept on reading.

After that she read all the *Signs* she could find and waited for the new ones to arrive. Then she heard about a series of lectures on Bible prophecy being held at the Milton-Freewater Seventh-day Adventist church. Julie attended, studied further, and was baptized. Later, she and her husband sold the tavern. It no longer held any interest for them.

"I can't imagine Julie drinking. Her face is so radiant with the love of Jesus. There are no traces of the old life left upon it," said Verna.

"She's trying to undo some of her past influence, too. Because of her experiences with alcohol and tobacco, she wants to spend the rest of her life helping people to conquer those habits. She's started with her old drinking friends," Lee observed.

"Yes, and they're listening, too," said Verna. "They can see the complete change in her way of life as well as in her appearance."

"I know that when we get a Story Hour started on the

reservation, Julie will want to help. She often saw how alcohol affected the Indians, and I've heard her talk about wanting to help them."

"That's right, Lee. I'm sure she will be one of our first volunteers if and when we can get a start on that reservation. They turned me down again today. I've got to think of another approach."

"They just don't think we will keep coming. We must prove it to them somehow, Verna."

Verna left the table and piled the dishes in the sink. Then, for some reason, she looked around her kitchen. It was full of pretty little things she had made. So was the whole house. She spoke one word.

"Crafts."

"Crafts?"

"Crafts," exclaimed Verna. "That's the answer. Indian children are naturally artistic. They work well with their hands. They respond to beauty. They have considerable free time after school every day. If we could gather materials to provide them with something to make with their hands, to decorate or paint, I believe they would come once a week. We wouldn't want to charge them anything for classes or materials. We could have classes all school year. The children get off the school bus near the long house. If I can just persuade the counselor . . ."

"Prayer can change things," reminded Lee as they sat down to have evening devotions. They both said, "Thank You, Lord," for this new idea.

CRAFTS AT THE LONG HOUSE

FIRST WE'LL SET UP tables and chairs in a corner of the long house and have craft materials spread out before the children arrive. As soon as they find their places and settle down a bit, I'll show them samples of the article we're making that day and tell them how to make it, then distribute the craft materials as they are needed. Then ——"

Verna's mind was racing with plans, as she once again drove determinedly toward the reservation. She mentally tossed out several carefully-rehearsed opening remarks she had ready for the counselor in favor of something direct and simple. The only thing I haven't tried with Ernie, she thought, is to pound his desk and have a tantrum. Maybe that would work.

She knew that the Indian agency had developed many new programs for Indian residents. A new attitude had developed in recent years, a growing pride in native American ancestry and heritage and a desire to revive long-lost customs and arts. East of the agency headquarters a new village unit was being built that would more adequately house many families. Another housing unit was in the planning stages. The proposed site for that was farther down the highway.

A new long house for socials and festivals adjoined recreation facilities near the village. Also in the planning stages were a new on-reservation school, and a clinic. An active alcohol and drug unit was attempting to make inroads in the almost universal drinking problem.

But nobody was holding crafts classes.

Wheeling into the parking lot, Verna found a space and was soon walking rapidly toward the alcohol and drug unit.

Ernie looked up as she came in.

"The word is still No," he said impassively.

"You haven't heard me——"

"I don't want to hear you."

"Crafts, Ernie. Let me have a crafts class for the school-age kids once a week in the long house."

"Crafts?" One black eyebrow raised.

"Crafts!"

"What would you do?"

Open Sesame!

A half hour later Verna was still telling him.

"And after crafts we'll have a rest period and play games before it's time to go home."

Ernie leaned forward in his chair.

"OK. I'll have to admit it sounds like a good program. Keep 'em off the streets. They need to learn to be constructive instead of destructive. What do you think, Garry?"

"Crafts? OK, I guess," said Garry.

"I'll designate you as a volunteer through this department, and you may have a class one day a week, in the gymnasium. I'll assign a man to help you set up tables and chairs and a woman volunteer to help keep order while you teach. One thing, though. You be here! Don't come a few times and get tired and leave. You're contracting to be here every Wednesday until school is out. This'll be on a strictly volunteer basis, and whatever expenses there are, you will pay, as you have said."

"Those are my terms exactly," said Verna, seriously.

As she turned to leave, she glanced back and grinned. "Oh, Ernie, I could hug you!"

"Umph," grunted Ernie.

Verna recruited a niece to help. Quickly they collected their materials and prepared for classes. There would be no charge for materials, and the children could take home whatever they made.

Soon Verna's crafts classes became a regular weekly feature. On most Wednesdays the children would rush from the school bus into the crafts room. They appeared hyperactive and were hard to handle at times, but were unusually adept at crafts and were always enthusiastic. Some days Verna had as many as 34 children. Once in a while, if there was a funeral or festival, no one would come. No one ever told her ahead of time, so she and her niece sometimes drove forty miles only to find that no children were coming.

Verna developed a varied crafts program. She was able to obtain considerable donated material to keep the children busy, but many of her supplies were bought from her own limited income. The children were eager to learn new skills and most of them were naturally artistic. They learned to mold candles with hot wax; they made cloth flowers, constructed a vase, cut out animal figures from carpet samples, and made many other things.

The building where Verna held classes also had office rooms. An outgoing, friendly person, she was appalled when she discovered that the people who worked there had nothing to say to her. In fact, they ignored her. Not only that, they looked right through her as if she were a windowpane when she smiled and said Hello. She was a "nothing."

The man who was designated to set up the tables for Verna began to talk to her a little. But the volunteer who helped to keep order would speak only in answer to a question. Sometimes Verna wished she had not promised to stay. But she did stay through the school year. She felt that God had given her the strength and courage. This was His program, not hers, for she had dedicated it to Him.

One day a young Indian man came to a busy crafts class. He quietly began setting up cameras and equipment. Verna realized that this was a videotape outfit. She decided to carry on the usual routine. Without explaining why he was there, he took pictures of the children during craft period and interviewed Verna, asking about the particular craft project they were doing at the time. Verna explained that materials used were all free to the children, and that when each project was completed, the child could take it home. She demonstrated to him how artistic the children were and how adept they were with their hands. The man looked surprised and pleased when she praised the children for their good work.

The photographer noticed the fuzzy animal figures cut from donated rug samples, and some of the items the children were making. He watched Verna's niece, with her flaming red hair, playing games with the children in the gymnasium after class. He filmed everything.

"Why are you coming out here and doing all this?" he asked Verna.

"Because I love them," she answered simply.

Verna doesn't know how many of the Indians saw that videotape. She only knows that the next week, when she went to the Indian village day-care center, everyone was suddenly very friendly. She was no longer to be "looked through" but to be accepted and spoken to. From then on she was free to go anywhere on the reservation.

God, with His own good timing, had opened another locked door. So Verna said, "Thank You, Lord," and began working on another obstacle.

FROM CRAFTS TO STORIES

ANY COMPROMISES or delays that Lee and Verna Clay appeared to accept were only temporary. Verna wanted a Story Hour, and she had been merely biding her time to achieve it.

But time was running out; the school year was nearly through. With the end of school, crafts classes would be over, the children scattered and gone. That is, unless—— Verna had another door to open.

"Time to open another door, Lord," she prayed.

After spending considerable earnest prayer time asking that she wouldn't be thrown out of the gymnasium, Verna quietly incorporated a trial Story Hour into one crafts period. Several carefully selected storytellers arrived. One woman brought some homing pigeons to show while she told the children about the history, care, and training of these birds, and of their strong homing instincts.

Nothing happened. In fact, the children loved the stories and clamored for more. Verna knew that all Indian children are natural story lovers, because for thousands of years tribal history and legends had been told and retold down through the generations in story form. They appreciate good, lively stories, for their ancient legends of heroes and animals are exciting and full of action.

Even though the days became longer and warmer, everyone hated to see the school year end. That would mean the end of crafts classes.

"Are you going to have crafts classes this summer?" Tilda asked.

"Not here," answered Verna. "We can be here only until school is out."

"O-o-oh," went a groan around the tables. "Why not?"

"No more stories, either?" frowned Jamie.

"Would you like to come to a whole week of crafts and stories this summer?" asked Verna. "There'll be songs and games, too."

"Ye-es!" yelled everybody. The children crowded around Verna, asking questions all at once. "Where? Where? You said it wouldn't be here!"

This was Verna's opportunity to tell them about summer Vacation Bible School and all the crafts and stories at Blue Mountain church.

"Would you like for me to come by and pick you up every morning and take you to Vacation Bible School? How many want to go?"

Of course everyone did.

The following week Verna brought folders advertising Vacation Bible School. She gave one to each child, saying, "Be sure to get your parents' permission to go."

Verna recruited Julie Overstreet from Weston, and together they visited as many homes as possible before Vacation Bible School time arrived, securing parental permission for children to attend the classes. This took a great deal of driving, for the Umatilla Indian Reservation covers many square miles.

Fortunately, by the time Vacation Bible School time came, Verna had gotten a large van. First, she picked up three or four children from her own neighborhood at Stateline, then drove down through Thornhollow into the reservation, picking up others along the way. Julie rode along to help. The van floor was carpeted, there were cushions to sit on, and what a merry ride they had. Some days it was pure bedlam. Sometimes they sang choruses all the way.

Having had little or no discipline at home, the Indian children liked to poke, punch, and spar with one another. They were noisy and giggly. Some of them were jittery from having had no breakfast before leaving home. They chose to miss a meal in order to meet the van on time, for Indian breakfasts are often delayed until nearly noon. As some of the parents drank nearly every night and slept most of the day, their youngsters had to fend for themselves and find whatever was cleanest to wear.

The children liked Vacation Bible School, although their behavior was sometimes disruptive. They grouped by themselves at first, and did not integrate easily with the white children. As some of the teachers found their behavior unacceptable, Verna had to go from kindergarten to primary to junior groups, restoring order and quelling small Indian uprisings here and there. On the final day the Indian girls brought the treats for the day, which everyone enjoyed.

For some time Lee and Verna had been attempting to arouse the interest of Darrell Perry, the new Blue Mountain church pastor, in their Indian project. He had told a story at one crafts class and had been at Vacation Bible School, but to become involved in any further way was about the last thing he wanted to do. He was busy with the needs of a growing, active church, and he was a cautious man.

He retained vivid memories of certain difficulties encountered years before during a former pastorate in South Dakota, at which time he had been involved with developing an on-reservation church and school in the Pine Ridge area, the only Seventh-day Adventist church and school building on reservation land in that part of the country. Land had been difficult to buy, and funds were nearly impossible to obtain. The work was slow and baptisms few.

Pastor Perry felt strongly that most Christian church groups had largely failed the American Indian population through the years because of the white man's concepts of conversion and demands for conformity. But because his own denomination had at that time formulated no definite guidelines or policies for evangelism among the Indians of North America, he hesitated to become a pioneer in the field with the little time he had to offer.

Not knowing the Clays well, he could not immediately assess their potential. They could only come under the category of plain, ordinary, unpretentious Christians, not outstanding in appearance, education, or worldly goods. And yet God had used them in a remarkable way in telling others about Jesus. Had it not been for that Story Hour in Weston years ago, he, Darrell Perry, might not be sitting behind his desk in this attractive little church office, developing a headache over the church budget. There probably wouldn't even be a Blue Mountain church if the Clays and several other dedicated families from Stateline hadn't persisted. A lot of people had come into the church through their efforts.

Pastor Perry believed that churches should reach out

and form new companies wherever possible. All things considered, there was little choice but to ask the Lord's guidance and seek to do His will. He knew that the Clays would be back.

A knock sounded on the door.

Here they were again.

All summer he had been too busy to listen. But he would listen now.

"Pastor, we feel we must find a place on the reservation to hold a Story Hour. Will you help us find one?"

"Next to impossible, you know," the Pastor shrugged, smiling a little to himself.

But the Clays had been seeing the impossible happen for a long time. "You know all things are possible with God."

"There's little or no money available to rent anything we may find."

"Ahh," Lee said with a smile. " 'My God shall supply all your need.' That includes even the Blue Mountain church budget. We'll find a way."

"Who's preaching to whom?" grinned Darrell Perry. "All right, I'll go with you to look for a place. Too late today; how about tomorrow?"

"We'll be there. Name your time."

Verna smiled all the way home. This door had been a little stiff, and squeaky on the hinges. But with the oil of the Holy Spirit, it was slowly swinging open. Verna knew that Pastor Perry, once committed, would be fully committed.

On a fine autumn day Lee and Verna Clay drove around the reservation with their pastor, looking for a place to rent so that they might begin a Story Hour. It couldn't be situated too far out in the hills, for gasoline prices were rising. There were many decaying and sagging buildings along the river, mostly not for rent and too far gone to salvage.

What were they to do?

Finally, upon inquiry, they learned that the Tillicum Grange Hall, situated in the middle of Mission, could sometimes be rented. Eventually they were able to negotiate to rent the hall every Saturday for $25 per week. There was one stipulation: A member of the Grange must be present each time it was used.

The Clays were excited and thankful that night as they knelt and gave praise for the Lord's leading.

Now came the work of planning a program and recruiting helpers. Lee and Verna could not run a Story Hour successfully without considerable volunteer help. Verna was soon dialing to ask Pastor Perry to send out announcements in the area, outlining the need for volunteers, supplies, donations, and many prayers for the success of the new program. In addition, the Clays contacted friends, asking them to volunteer time each week or to come occasionally as they were able. Many volunteered, some to help for a short time, others to stay on month after month.

Julie Overstreet wondered if she had time to continue with the program. Finally she telephoned Verna.

"I've had a battle, but the Lord reminded me that I have wanted to be a missionary, especially to those who have an alcohol or drug problem. I could almost hear Him say, 'OK, Julie, here's your chance; either put up or shut up.' This project will be real mission work. I'll be there to help."

"Praise the Lord!" Verna exclaimed.

In summer the Umatilla Reservation lies baked and dusty as the burning winds howl over the hills, picking up dust and momentum. Fallow grain fields lose inches of topsoil as it swirls, powderfine, into the air to mingle with other soil from the western desert land along the great Columbia River.

As the days shorten and cool, the summer winds give way to fall breezes. The air becomes bright and crisp, and there is a tinge of frost in early morning. Along the Umatilla River, which winds through the reservation, the multitudes of tall, spreading cottonwoods put on their breathtaking display of yellow and gold, first on the outermost tips, then spreading downward as sharp and yet sharper frosts come, until each tree stands out completely gold against a warm blue sky.

Thorn apples and chokecherries, in an effort to outdo their larger cousins, turn scarlet and purple. The fall daisies bloom higher up in the hills, adding their pink-blue tones to the overwhelming kaleidoscopic farewell to summer.

Beyond the blue foothills, as they merge with mauve mountain slopes, the Umatilla River grows smaller. Cottonwood gold begins to mingle with aspen yellow before a background of dark pine forest.

When autumn was well under way on the reservation that year a group of lively children gathered in the little Tillicum Grange Hall each Sabbath morning to hear stories of Jesus and His love.

IT'S HIS PROGRAM

STEVEN AND CARMEN McWilliams were tired but excited. On this perfect September day after traveling all the way across the nation from Pittsburgh, Pennsylvania, they were now cruising along the freeway that cuts straight through the Blue Mountains of eastern Oregon.

"These mountains aren't as high as some we've seen, but the pines are pretty," Carmen commented, gazing at the pine-covered ridges and steep canyons sweeping away on both sides of them. When I came to Walla Walla College for spring quarter I flew, and didn't see much of the surrounding countryside."

"Deadman's Pass," chuckled Steve, noticing a road sign. "These Western names certainly appeal to the imagination. I wonder what hapless hombre this spot was named for?"

"Oh, let's stop at the overlook ahead," exclaimed Carmen suddenly. "It looks as if we could see for a long way."

The car slowly came to a stop in the parking area. Steve got out and stretched his tall frame. Every muscle in his body felt tired. He hopped about a bit to encourage the circulation in his legs, ran a hand over his Afro-styled hair, and yawned. "Believe me," he declared, "this is one fella who will be glad to reach his destination!"

Already looking over the rim of the canyon into the vast valley, Carmen, map in hand, was intrigued by the unique multihued checkerboard effect of the fields that stretched away as far as the September afternoon haze would allow them to see.

Pointing to a body of water to the southwest, she said, "That must be McKay Reservoir."

"And that's Pendleton, with all the smoke, due west. Looks like it's built in a canyon."

"We're on the Umatilla Reservation already; it began several miles back, according to the sign," said Carmen, still poring over the map. "It's quite large."

"Which way is College Place?"

"Well, let's see." Carmen pointed a slim brown finger at the map. "We're here. The road turns north before we come to Pendleton, and then it's about forty miles."

She turned her wide brown eyes toward her husband and smiled sweetly. "Poor dear, you're exhausted driving all these miles without a break. Shall I take a turn and give you a little rest?"

Steve grinned down at his slim, lovely young wife. "It's not far now; I can make it."

They turned once more to the view. Fields once green were now gold, and the blend of colors appealed to Carmen, who had much talent as an artist. The lowering sun, and the haze which filtered it's rays, softened the harsh, treeless landscape before them.

"We've seen a lot of the wide-open spaces of the West already, haven't we? No hardwood forests here. And I can tell you, the climate is as changeable as the landscape," said Carmen.

"After the beautiful wooded hills around Oakwood College, I expect Walla Walla College will really be a change. But it seems to be the place for you to complete your art major, while I apply to work for the State." Steve smiled. "Let's go. Destiny awaits."

As Steve and Carmen drove through the little community of Mission, on the Umatilla Reservation, Carmen exclaimed, "Oh, there are some Indians!"

"Come, come," laughed Steve. "They're not the first Indians you've seen."

"But on a reservation . . . " Carmen began.

"Don't forget, young lady, I may not show it, but my mother is part Cherokee. That's the secret of my being so handsome."

"Oh, you're becoming worse by the mile!" Carmen gave her husband a little nudge and laughed.

"Seriously, I wonder if our church is doing anything on this reservation and who's working here. I'd like to become involved, working for the Indians, wouldn't you?" asked Steve.

"Maybe we can." Carmen settled back as the road wound around a hill and straightened out again.

Several miles farther, on the outskirts of a small town called Athena, Carmen said, "Look! Blue Mountain Seventh-day Adventist church. Right here on the highway. Looks like a nice little place."

In Milton-Freewater they saw another new, larger, modern-styled Adventist church.

"Must be a lot of Adventists in this area," said Steve. "The towns don't look all that big."

A few miles farther Carmen said, "Here's our turnoff. That sign is easy to miss: 'Walla Walla College. Kindly turn left.'"

In the gathering darkness they drove up tree-lined College Avenue, and Steve gazed at the campus and buildings. "'Walla Walla College. Established 1892,'" he read from the sign that hung by the side of the road.

"So this," proclaimed Steve, "is your future alma mater!"

"A lot of work between now and then," muttered Carmen. "I'm glad I was able to find a place for us when I was out here for spring quarter. The Cowins were really nice to keep it for us through the summer."

After moving into their apartment the young couple became absorbed in work and study. Carmen pursued her art major and Steve went to work at Harris Pine Mills in Pendleton for several months while his application to work at Washington State Penitentiary was being processed. After a few months Steve became a counselor in the maximum security unit in the prison.

Steve and Carmen had been in College Place only a few days when Mrs. Cowin stopped by to ask them if they would perhaps be interested in doing a little missionary work.

"I've been hoping we could find a place to witness, with the Lord's help," exclaimed Steve. "What do you have in mind?"

"Mr. and Mrs. Clay, friends of ours, are searching for young Christian couples to help with the weekly Story Hour to be held on the Umatilla Reservation. And," added Mrs. Cowin, "I told them I had an idea you'd be interested."

"We certainly are!" answered Steve and Carmen together.

Verna Clay was on their doorstep in no time at all, it seemed. Carmen invited her in.

She settled into a comfortable chair and got right to the point.

"We're organizing a Story Hour for the Indian children on the Umatilla Reservation, and we are looking for people to help us. We need storytellers, teachers for classes, someone to lead in singing, to help gather up the children, to visit the families in their homes, and an endless list of other things. This is a new venture. We need competent help; we can't do it all alone."

"You mean to tell me that there's been no work done for the Indians on this reservation by our church?" Steve was incredulous.

Verna shook her head. "Not up to now."

Carmen leaned forward in her chair. "Isn't this strange? We were wondering about our work on the reservation when we first came here," she said eagerly, "and hoping we might become involved with the program as volunteers."

"It's just a beginnning," explained Verna. "Don't expect too much. We have been years in making even a little progress. This is all volunteer work. You will find it challenging. You may find it thankless at times, but rewarding in other ways. Would you like to help us pioneer?"

Steve laughed. "Well, are you going to have an evangelist come in and hold meetings?"

"No," replied Verna, "we're working with a minority group having a tightly closed social structure. Nobody would come to meetings like that."

"I know something about the problems of minority groups, having grown up in Pittsburgh and graduated from Oakwood College. I am not only black, but part Cherokee," Steve said with a smile. "Tell us more, Mrs. Clay."

"The two churches that attempted to Christianize the Indians have long ago ceased to work actively for them. And the Indians are not particularly welcome when they go into the churches in town. Alcohol has pretty well taken the place of religion. Teen-agers not only drink but also blow their minds with drugs. Long assocation with white people has convinced them that whites are not to be trusted.

"The Indians do not trust the white man's religion altogether, either, because they feel the white's can't even agree among themselves on certain doctrines. Out of this has grown a modern-day combination of parts of Christianity and parts of the old Indian religious beliefs and customs that suit many of them very well. They want no change unless they can see results. Therefore we have to live among them to be living proof that they can see and understand.

"There is little justice in the courts for Indians, and often when one dies by violence or accident, the case is not investigated thoroughly. It's been a hundred years since the last Indian uprising, but unfortunately the attitude still prevails among some local whites that the only good Indian is a dead Indian. Of course there are individuals who feel different, but they are in the minority.

"Indians who live on the reservation have little going for them, little chance to better themselves. There have been few successful programs to provide job incentives or job readiness. Local prejudice precludes job availability, and the ambitious Indian who wants an education and a job has to leave the reservation to obtain it.

"Then he faces another problem," continued Verna. "Having once left the reservation, he is no longer welcome to return to his people; he finds not only white prejudice but ostracism from his own tribe. Regarding family ties as highly as he does, the average Indian simply doesn't want to take the risk, so he shifts into neutral and coasts through the rest of his life on Government handouts."

"In other words we should not try to change the

Indians to the point of forcing them into our culture mold," said Steve thoughtfully, "because they have their own ways of thinking and doing, and our ways could offend them."

"Exactly," said Verna. "At this point we don't know their customs, and in our ignorance we often offend. But they are forgiving, once they understand that although many of our ways are basically different, we are not out to change their customs but to learn and respect those customs."

Steve leaned back, stretched his long legs, then sat up straight.

"Yes, we would like to be a part of this work. We don't have much time to devote to it, but we can come on weekends. I'm sure it will be a learning experience for both of us.

"I've been reading several books along the line of how much we owe to our fellowmen," Steve continued. "We willingly send missionaries overseas. That's great. But how much time do we spend on missionary work at home? It may not be glamorous, but aren't these Indians as precious in God's eyes as anyone overseas? It sounds as if God's people have not done what they should be doing."

"With Jesus' coming so near, that's frightening," said Carmen. "Someone will be held accountable for work not done."

"God must have known we'd have this opportunity," Steve observed. "He prepares us for things. I sold books door to door before coming here. The Lord helped me overcome my fear of knocking on doors, even after I had guns held on me several times. He gives us strength to perform whatever task He wishes us to do."

"We found long ago that Satan opposes any new work," said Verna. "We can only offer God's free salvation, and then ask the Holy Spirit to be in control and make the best of our feeble efforts."

"God is waiting for us to trust Him," declared Steve. "He'll lead us. It's His program."

And so they knelt in a prayer of rededication, asking for the power of the Holy Spirit and praising God for His leading in love.

MISSION IN THEIR OWN BACK YARD

SITTING IN THEIR accustomed place in the Pendleton Seventh-day Adventist church, Juanita leaned toward her husband and whispered, "Can you hear that announcement?"

Ken was hard of hearing and sometimes missed a lot of information. He looked at Juanita and nodded, then turned to listen to the speaker.

"Volunteers are urgently needed to help with the weekly Story Hour for Indian children, held at the Tillicum Grange in Mission. Someone is needed to help pick up children. Many volunteers are needed to come out week by week to help with this program. Anyone willing to help, please call Lee or Verna Clay at ——"

Ken stared straight ahead until the announcement was over. He looked thoughtful during the remainder of church.

"I wonder if they'd let us bring some of our neighbor children. They're not Indian, but they sure like stories," he mused.

As soon as they were out of church, walking toward

their car, Ken said, "Juanita, let's call the Clays. I think we could find a few children to take to Story Hour right in our own neighborhood."

"Of course we could; there's a multitude of them all around us with nothing to do on Saturdays," answered Juanita quickly.

"You've always wanted to be a missionary," Ken grinned shyly, "and ——"

"And here's my chance, huh? Well, I wonder if my being an eighth Chippewa would help in working with these Indians"

Driving home, Juanita thought how ironic it all was. Now that she was a grandmother, retired and ill, here might be her chance to be a missionary. Life was strange. It had always been. Her mind roamed back over the years.

When she was a small child, she had loved to hear the adventure stories of her great-grandfather, a Chippewa chief, who had married the platinum-blonde daughter of settlers. Juanita had always been proud to be part Chippewa.

Problems in her home had made it necessary for her to spend many years growing up in a foster home, away from her family. One day a colporteur came along selling a book called *Bible Readings for the Home*. Her foster father bought a copy. Juanita was fascinated by the book, and began to spend many hours studying it and reading the Bible verses listed under each subject. Many nights, when other girls were dating, she stayed at home to read that book. Seeing her interest in it, her foster parents eventually gave it to her.

When Ken Cripe came along, Juanita was attracted to this good-looking, considerate young man, and in time they were married. Neither one belonged to any particular church, but Ken and Juanita felt they should establish a church affiliation along with the establishment of their home.

They spent much time discussing which church they should join. Somehow, they could not quite decide. This one was too radical, another seemed too conservative.

One day as they were talking Ken said suddenly, "I could prove to you from the Bible that the Seventh-day Adventist Church is right if I just had a certain book."

"What book is that?"

"It's called *Bible Readings for the Home.*"

"Could you, now?" Juanita answered with a smile. She rose quickly and vanished into the bedroom. Coming out shortly, she walked briskly over to Ken and handed him a book.

"Well, let's see you do it," she challenged, laughing at the surprised, pleased look spreading over his face.

For several months Ken and Juanita studied, going over each subject, looking up texts, and marking them in their Bibles. As soon as they felt they were prepared to make a commitment, Ken found the name of the local Seventh-day Adventist church pastor and called to make an appointment.

When they asked the surprised minister for baptism, he began to ask them questions. He found that they could answer each one correctly from the Bible.

They were soon baptized without any further studies.

Ken worked as an electrician for many years. Juanita was a cook at the local State hospital. Shortly before retiring they moved to Shenandoah Estates, a comfortable urban area with modest middle-class homes. They anticipated a quiet life. Then Ken's hearing began to deteriorate to the point that he had to wear an aid in each ear. Over the years Juanita developed a heart problem, as well as a bone disorder that caused her much pain.

The Cripes could have easily settled into a slow-paced

retirement routine after their busy working years, for Ken and Juanita had developed many interests and hobbies. Juanita loved house plants, cooking was her specialty, and she was an equally enthusiastic seamstress.

For years there had been a long-buried desire to be missionaries deep inside both of them. But they had forgotten it long, long ago, knowing it was impossible. With retirement, however, they wondered if there might not be a project in which they could participate. Ken still worked part time at electrical jobs. He wasn't satisfied with sitting around all day.

Believing they could be useful in the Story Hour program, Ken and Juanita voluteered to help. The Clays were certainly in need of assistance. After circulating the news about Story Hour among the children and parents of his neighborhood, Ken started bringing children. Before long he had a vanload of ten or fifteen coming each week.

During Story Hour Ken and Juanita helped the children find Bible verses and often sat with them to show them how to listen. Juanita found that the children responded eagerly to her love. They were hungry for attention and respected her when she would say, "This is the right way; do it this way." Kids clambered all over Ken, and often he could be seen with a child on each knee while stories were being told.

The Cripes' association with the Story Hour group was a learning experience. Ken and Juanita found that the Indian children had a smattering of Bible knowledge, but that their theology was a mixed bag of Protestant and Catholic beliefs. During the early days of the reservation the Catholic Church established St. Andrews Mission, dedicated to converting the Indians living on the north side of the Umatilla River. The Presbyterians held forth on the south side of the river, with their mission and the church at Tutuilla. By the 1960s both missions had nearly ceased to exist. Although the Catholic academy closed for lack of students, the Catholic mission did not close entirely. It is still situated in a sheltered fold of hills and is manned by a limited staff.

Alcoholism, Juanita discovered, had been a major factor in the breakup of family life and the ruin of several generations of Indians since the coming of the whites. More recently the Indian population had taken to drugs as avidly as their predecessors had taken to alcohol. One could see that the parents of the Story Hour children were virtually a lost generation. Forced into confined reservation living, years of substandard housing, and government handouts, the native people gave up in despair and apathy. With new, improved government housing, they lived rent-free, to a great extent, and depended on welfare, occasional government grants, annual rental funds for croplands leased to whites, and food stamps, which were used to get liquor, albeit illegally. Having been taught little about discretion or thrift and having no concept of how to budget time or money, they provided poorly for their families and just scraped by.

When Juanita went visiting she encountered difficulty finding anyone at home. She discovered that many children were cared for by grandparents because the parents assumed little responsibility for any phase of living. Children were left to their own devices, and were often undernourished from the junk food they ate and love-starved from parental neglect.

One day several of the Story Hour volunteers were discussing ways and means of reaching older children, teens, and adults.

"We're finding that Indian youth start drinking early

and are often alcoholics by fifteen or sixteen," explained Lee Clay.

"Several of our foster children have been alcoholics and almost impossible to help," added Verna.

"When children reach a certain age they lose interest and stop coming to the Story Hour. We must do something to keep their interest or we'll have yet another generation of alcoholics," said Julie Overstreet. "The older children turn naturally to the drugs and alcohol their parents use so freely. I know how alcohol affects them. I saw enough of that during the years I owned a tavern. Believe me, we've got to do more than we're doing."

"There's another problem," said Verna. "The rich cultural heritage of the local tribes is rapidly being lost because of apathy and lack of interest by both Indians and whites. The languages and tribal customs are dying out with the older generation. Only a few speak the native tongue anymore, and the old legends are being lost. Even interest in their special crafts is diminishing."

Steve McWilliams, who had been listening carefully, said, "We know that evangelism as Carmen and I have known it is not effective with a group such as the Umatillas. This type of culture has to be approached differently. One must meet them at their level, and be accepting of their ways of thinking. We must offer them something that interests them."

Juanita Cripe, a practical person observed, "It's plain to see in visiting with adults on this reservation that the Indian women are interested in cooking classes. I believe they would come if we had a place to hold such classes. I'd be willing to help teach them if we only had a building or something. We can't do it here in the Grange."

"Nor in the long house," added Verna. "These women want to learn to knit and crochet, to sew and make quilts. We must have a building. When I have suggested to the Indian women that they could teach to the others the crafts that they know well, such as beadwork, buckskin crafts, and basketry, they have been pleased and excited at the possibility."

"Classes of this type," said Pastor Perry, "would undoubtedly draw of lot of Indians who are repelled by the white man's sometimes confusing religion."

We could do all these things," Lee Clay summarized, "if we had a place of our own with classrooms."

"We must find a way," agreed Pastor Perry, "although I know too well the problems we may encounter."

"The Lord has led us this far. He'll provide again," said Lee.

All the way home from Story Hour Juanita kept thinking, All these years, and I had a mission field in my own back yard.

BLACK, RED, AND WHITE

WINTER ON THE reservation can be a dismal experience. The winds blow sharp and cold, howling through poorly insulated buildings and driving the heat right on through.

A skim of snow occasionally decorates the acres of stubble left after the wheat harvest. Temperatures drop to -20°F without warning. Roads and highways sometimes become sheets of ice, and cars slide hopelessly about. Alternate freezing and thawing make unpaved roads impassable. But Indian children appear impervious to cold and play outdoors, often poorly clad, even in bitter weather.

But spring comes early on the sunny slopes. Like a soft-eyed Indian maiden, she strews myriads of wild flowers on the brown hills, lingers to warm the slopes, then climbs, melting the snow line ever higher. The Umatilla River becomes a wild, excited thing, overflowing with snow melt. Gradually the trees take on a green tint. Nature and its creatures respond joyfully to the surge of new life all around.

All winter and spring Story Hour had been going fairly well. Some weeks there were forty children, sometimes only a few. The volunteers found that the Indians put their own cultural activities first, as might be expected.

Steve McWilliams found himself doing things he never dreamed of doing, one of which was leading the children in singing. Carmen wrote out a number of lively choruses on sheets of cardboard, and rivalry was strong among the younger children when it came time to hold the words for everyone to see. Steve worked it so that each child might have his turn holding the cards. Sometimes Russell Coleman came over from College Place to play the piano for them. How the children loved to sing! They seemed to be naturally musical and quickly learned the words and melodies of many choruses.

Carmen taught the weekly Bible story to the kindergarten-age children. This suited her just right. They loved her and she loved them. She was able to put her artistic talents to work, making lesson illustrations for the flannel board, providing pictures for the children to color, and sometimes making tiny booklets for the children to take home.

Every week each child received a copy of *Our Little Friend, Primary Treasure,* or *Guide* to take home. These papers were provided by the members of the Blue Mountain church, as were the *Signs* and other papers to be distributed to the adults.

Each of the volunteers continued to beg any friend who would listen to come to Story Hour and tell stories to the children, whose story appetites seemed insatiable.

One day Steve brought a black woman to Story Hour. Now, Steve and Carmen are not very dark, not much darker than the Indian children, in fact. But this woman visitor was really dark. One little boy, Jimmy, stared at her in astonishment and dislike all during the singing and throughout the story. Verna, who always sat with the children to keep order during the story, noticed that Jimmy seemed to be upset by something. But he didn't say anything until the children separated for their Bible lessons. Then he walked right up to the visitor and blurted out, "I don't like you, lady; your face is dirty."

Racial prejudice had reared its ugly head right in the middle of Story Hour!

With a despairing, apologetic shake of her head toward the slightly taken-aback visitor, Verna took Jimmy by the hand and led him to the class. There she gave him and his friends a description of the different races of men and their differing shades of color. She explained that some were red, like Jimmy, some were white, like Tammy, some were yellow, brown, and, yes, black. She explained that nobody should be ashamed of his race or color, nor should anyone be overly proud of his color, either, because in God's sight all races of men on this earth are brothers and should treat one another as equals.

Jimmy listened. The children asked questions. They had a good discussion. Jimmy now realized he had probably hurt the woman's feelings, so after class, as the children were leaving, he ran to the visitor, looked up into her kind, smiling face and said, "Sorry, lady, sorry, lady!" and ran out the door to jump into the van for the ride home.

One day in May, Verna Clay drove into Walla Walla to purchase a birthday present for a relative. She was driving through an intersection with the green light in her favor when an automobile hurtled through the red light, crashed broadside, into her vehicle and pushed it violently against the curb.

For a few stunned moments Verna sat immobilized.

The crash had happened so fast and so unexpectedly! She turned off the ignition and tried to open the door, but it was stuck fast. She leaned over to try to open the door on the passenger side and found that it would not open. Then, as she began to move around, she discovered that her knee hurt. Something was wrong with her back, too. When she turned her head, she knew she was in trouble. Her neck really hurt.

As people began to gather and police drove up and pushed their way through Verna sat and groaned. She was on such a busy schedule, with all she had to do today, and now this! She groaned again. How was she going to get out?

Suddenly, the back door was wrenched open from the outside, and Verna felt a kind hand on her shoulder. A familiar voice said, "Verna, are you all right? Let me help."

She glanced in the direction of the voice. It was a longtime friend of the Clays, Hal Larson.

"The Lord must have sent you," she exclaimed. "I'm not all right, and you can help."

RESTING IN GOD'S ARMS

CRAWLING TO THE back seat with Hal's help, Verna pulled herself from the damaged vehicle. But when she tried to stand, her knee gave way, and she gave a sharp cry of pain.

"You're going to a doctor right now, to see about that knee," declared Hal firmly.

"Oh, no——" Verna started to remonstrate.

"Come on, you're in no condition to argue. I'll take you to the doctor. Then I'll call your daughter, and she can come to get you."

The X-rays revealed nothing seriously wrong, so Verna returned to normal activity after the bruises and soreness healed.

She continued to experience headaches. Several weeks later she visited a doctor, who ordered cervical X-rays. She had had a cervical fusion several years before, and X-rays revealed that the fusion had been damaged. The doctor recommended a refusion.

So three months after the accident Verna entered a hospital. After a series of thorough examinations, the doctor explained his findings to Lee and Verna. "There appears to be no way to relieve the pain without surgery. Prolonged immobilization is not enough. In this situation it would be best to stabilize the area by fusing. In order to do this we will have to go in through the front. No surgical procedure is entirely without risk, but this should be fairly routine."

Verna, recalling her previous fusion, listened to the doctor's explanation. Her eyes welled with tears as he described the type of surgery that would have to be done. She knew the routine already.

"I don't look forward to this," she sighed, "but I don't enjoy all this pain, either."

"I have scheduled you for surgery day after tomorrow."

The day of surgery came all too soon. From the recovery room Verna was taken to the intensive care unit. Something had gone wrong. She couldn't swallow. Instead of getting better she became weaker. People swam in and and out of her vision. Sometimes, when she was half conscious, she felt as though she were spinning through clouds. She tried to pray, but the thought kept coming into her mind that this time the devil was winning. Where was God?

Lee stayed with her as much as possible. Her daughter came to be with her. Verna appeared to have lost the will to live. Lee talked with the doctor, who admitted that during surgery the surgeon had accidentally made a hole in Verna's esophagus. Within a few days an abscess formed in her throat.

Verna was not expected to live. Two weeks after surgery she was still failing. More abscesses formed in her throat and one lung collapsed. Very little was being done for her. It seemed useless.

Finally her daughter, who felt that her mother might

recover if more care were provided, had a long talk with the doctor. He decided to do more surgery through herback to clear out the infection, which was now in her lungs. He continued to treat the infection in her throat. By this time Verna had been unconscious for several days, feverish, and packed in ice.

With intensive treatment, the infection disappeared, the fever came down a little, and Verna regained consciousness. She felt terrible pain and still couldn't swallow, and the places where she had been cut were raw and sore. Her back was bound up, but it had to be cleaned every day. Now, she was aware most of the time and felt that Satan was trying to kill her. As days faded into weeks she did not improve.

The pain was too much. Injections helped a little, but her nerves were weak, and she wanted to scream with the pain. She couldn't seem to pray. Nobody really expected her to live, but she didn't want to die. She kept seeing Mara's face. Her Indian children! She wanted to live for her Indian children!

One nurse seemed really concerned. She would sit for as long as she could and hold Verna's hand, talking softly. Verna couldn't pray, but the kindly nurse could, and Verna was grateful.

"There's a time for you to rest completely in the arms of God," she told Verna. "Be at peace in His will."

Finally Verna was well enough to be able to think about what to do. Why hadn't she thought about it before? It seemed impossible for her to recover, but she would be anointed and know God's will for her life.

Lee agreed. He was nearly exhausted from trying to keep up with everything. He had prayed constantly, but his prayers seemed to be bound with chains.

One afternoon Lee, Pastor Perry, and Elder Fralick from the Milton-Freewater church, came to the hospital.

Verna and Lee yielded their wills and plans to God and claimed His promises. The day after Verna was anointed her throat infection appeared to be gone. She was far from well, but within a week she was out of the hospital and convalescing at home. That took six more weeks. As she grew stronger she spent most of her time studying and reading her Bible.

While it was time for Verna to rest, it was time for others to grow. Each week Julie Overstreet continued to pick up as many children for Story Hour as she could. She taught, told stories, and visited when time allowed. Steve and Carmen came to help, although their time was limited. All the volunteers worked hard to keep the program going, knowing that Verna might not live to come back. All felt depressed as weeks went by.

One Sabbath not one child came to Story Hour. Julie was in tears. The volunteers sat in a corner of the empty Grange hall to discuss what to do. Maybe this was the end. Perhaps they should quit. Possibly this wasn't God's program.

Steve was quiet. He sat thoughtfully, listening. Suddenly he jumped to his feet and said, "Let's not get discouraged, even though things look bad. The Lord brought us together for some reason today. Let's praise Him. We're coming again next Sabbath."

"You're right, Steve," said Julie. "We'll be here."

And they were—with a room full of children.

"It's His program," said Steve. "Praise the Lord!"

After Story Hour he delivered to Verna a batch of get-well wishes from "her" little Indians.

That did her as much good as any medicine.

One day she came again to Story Hour, weak but walking. How happy she was to see them all again, swarming about her like little wild bees!

GOOD, BAD, AND DIFFERENT

THE CLAYS SOON found that the Grange, although it was on reservation land, was basically a white man's place. So, except for mothers and grandmothers, who came on special occasions, few other Indians came. But they allowed the children to come. The children were excited, lively, and noisy during Story Hour. Lee and Verna were accustomed to this, but some visitors were horrified at "so much noise." They sometimes complained, asking why the children were not taught to sit still and be reverent. After all, this was the Sabbath, and a worship service, for all intents and purposes.

How could Verna help the visitors to understand what Indian children go through every day?

Finally she took one of the objecting visitors aside. "Do you see that boy over there?" she said. "His mother was stabbed last week. He's distressed and confused. He doesn't know what's going to happen to him. He can't handle it. His brother and sister over there are four and five. They are all staying with their grandmother, and they are afraid. They receive no love or training at all.

The whole thing is too much for them.

"And do you see those two children over there? Their mother has been drunk for more than a week. Last week I had to hold them because they were near tears all during Story Hour. When I went to get them I saw broken glass and blood all over the floor. Today, on the way to Story Hour, little Ted said, 'My mother's going to kill herself.' He paused, looked tearful, then angry, and said, 'Well, let her!'

"The broken glass and blood hasn't been cleaned up yet. Some children say they hate to go home because they know that there will be drinking and fighting going on, and no food."

The visitor turned pale. "Oh," she faltered, shaken, "I guess I didn't understand."

In addition to the Story Hour, Verna, Julie, and several volunteers distributed *Signs of the Times* on the reservation, visiting with the families as much as they were allowed and inviting the adults to visit Story Hour with their children.

One woman told them that she would never come because she was satisfied with her own religion, but she appreciated what her children were learning. They were better behaved, and even their grades in school were improving.

Trial and error seemed to be the name of the game. Not knowing the Indian customs, the Clays sometimes made mistakes. Once, during a friendly visit, their host offered them some choice bits of smoked salmon. As Lee politely declined the delicacy, he was dismayed to see the man's face cloud over with disappointment. He was hurt deeply at this refusal of hospitality. The Clays began to realize that Indians consider it rude for a visitor to refuse food offered to him. To eat is a token of friendship. To refuse is an insult.

A few Indian families allowed the Clays to give them Bible studies, but said they preferred to keep their own religion.

The volunteers smiled ruefully at some of the setbacks. At times they felt that Satan had won a round. But they clung to the promise that Satan had been defeated at the cross, and they renewed their faith, believing that God would overrule even when their motives were misinterpreted.

In spite of new Federal housing, many of the Indians still lived in fearfully inadequate shacks, poorly wired, and heated with flimsy old wood heaters. Fires in dwellings were frequent. The Story Hour group tried to be aware of these disasters and to respond quickly with bedding, clothing, and household goods. Local church community services groups donated generously, and the Clays were able to obtain chests of drawers and other furniture from the Harris Pine Mills. They found that the Indians were not greedy and took only what they absolutely needed.

Among the first group of children to come to Story Hour were several young teen-agers. Because the program was geared to younger children, these older ones eventually lost interest and quit coming. The volunteers could see a desperate need to expand their program to include material for older children. They wanted to start a Pathfinder program, but, again, they were hampered by lack of adequate facilities. There were not enough volunteers. The need was growing too fast for the group to handle.

PRAISE HIM ANYWAY!

LEE AND VERNA often looked about the reservation, hoping to find a place to live. They had decided that the only way to win the confidence of the adult Indians was to move to the reservation, live among them, be friendly with them, and learn their ways. They must show respect to traditional Indian customs while living among them, but teach and demonstrate a better way. The Clays knew that they would have to show by their daily lives the love of Jesus and how He can change lives. So they prayed that the Lord would show them where He wanted them to be, for they could see that the Indians needed a new way of life.

One day, during Story Hour, Verna casually glanced out a front window. Directly cross the road was a "For Sale" sign.

She took a second look. No, her eyes weren't deceiving her. There was a nice house and garage, with a few acres of land, for sale.

It can't be, she thought.

"But it is!" she exclaimed out loud.

Hearing her, Lee walked over to where Verna sat gazing spellbound out the window. "Did you call me?" he asked.

"Look," she responded. "Was that sign there when we first came?"

"What sign?" queried Lee.

"Look out the window. Across the street," said Verna. "See the 'For Sale' sign?"

Lee looked, astonished. He stood a long while before he spoke. "Maybe that's the Lord's answer," he said softly.

Sabbath or not, Story Hour or not, they couldn't help looking, just a little. In fact, it was hard to concentrate on anything else.

"What a perfect location," Lee exclaimed, as Story Hour ended and the children ran out to the van.

"Right in the heart of the reservation," Verna exulted.

"Let's make this the subject of special prayer until Monday morning," suggested Lee as they drove away.

Verna glanced back once more. "Oh, I can hardly wait until Monday morning, can you? Wouldn't this be the most ideal spot on the whole reservation? Right here in Mission, almost next door to the agency and the village."

Monday morning finally came. Lee and Verna were at the real estate office as soon as it opened; the property had not been sold. The realtor took them out to Mission and showed it to them. They went over it thoroughly. The situation and amount of land was ideal. Many years before, the property had been divided into four separate tax lots and zoned for a church and school.

Incredible!

The Clays were walking around as if in a dream. The Lord had planned this, years ago, long before they ever thought of living on the reservation. And here it was for sale at exactly the right time. In addition to the house and garage there were a few outbuildings, a large garden spot, and good water from a well.

"This has to be from the Lord," they said to each other, and promptly put down a deposit.

Then they went to the Indian Agency office at Mission to double-check on the zoning to see if the agency would tentatively approve their donating two of the lots for a church building.

"No problem," replied the man at the agency. "I'm sure the Tribal Council will approve the sale of the land to you. Later, when the property is yours, come see me about the building. I'll let you know the decision of the Tribal Council regarding the sale of the property."

The days went by and Lee and Verna eagerly waited to have the sale completed. They received tribal approval, but other matters delayed the signing of the final papers.

One day they received a long-awaited call from the real estate office.

"I'm sorry to tell you . . . that is . . . this will be very disappointing for you," stammered the real estate agent. "I know how much you have wanted the property in Mission, but——"

"But what?" Lee asked with a sudden sinking feeling.

"The owner of that property has died unexpectedly, before he signed the final papers, and I've been notified that the property has gone into an estate. It may be a long time before it's free to sell. The heirs are in disagreement."

Lee found it hard to tell Verna. Disappointed, she burst into tears.

That night at family worship they prayed, "Lord, show us what we need to learn; give us patience. Let us not run before Thee. Overrule this situation to Thy glory and not ours. This is Thy work, and we have dedicated ourselves to Thee. We thank Thee for leading us thus far."

"This is a testing time, Verna," said Lee. "I believe God wants to be sure that we understand what our commitment is. In suffering or in testing, man can be a window, reflecting God's love to others. Sometimes to experience adversity is an honor. This shows that in spite of strong temptations God feels He can trust us to abide in Him and to praise Him anyway."

Together they read James 1:2-6, so appropriate to their feelings, so applicable to their situation: "'My brethren, count it all joy when ye fall into divers temptations; knowing this, that the trying of your faith worketh patience. But let patience have her perfect work, that ye may be perfect and entire, wanting nothing. If any of you lack wisdom, let him ask of God, that giveth to all men liberally, and upbraideth not; and it shall be given him. But let him ask in faith, nothing wavering.'"

"Praise Him anyway!" mused Verna. "That's exactly what Paul means in Philippians 4:6, 7, isn't it? 'Be careful for nothing; but in every thing by prayer and supplication with thanksgiving let your requests be made known unto God. And the peace of God, which passeth all understanding, shall keep your hearts and minds through Jesus Christ.'"

"With promises like that, we can certainly trust God to work things out," said Lee. "Let's be sure that His trust in us isn't misplaced. We must be channels of His love, reflectors of His glorious light."

Even so, it was hard to go to Story Hour each week after that and look across the road at what had almost been theirs.

FOR SALE!
TO ANYBODY BUT US

LEE AND VERNA continued to haunt the real estate agency, which had little progress to report. One of the heirs, knowing something about what the Clays wanted to do with part of the acreage, objected. He did not want to sell the land to them. He felt that his own church should be the only group working with Indians.

So the land went back on the market. The house stood empty, the weeds began to grow tall, and the grass and shrubs went uncared for. Lee and Verna did not wish to accuse anyone of discrimination, but it appeared that the property was for sale to anyone but them. They waited to see what would happen.

Nothing happened. No one came to buy.

One day, when the Clays arrived for the Story Hour, a policeman was walking about the yard of the house. They crossed the street to ask him what was happening. He explained that vandals had recently broken in and had done some damage. He was routinely examining the evidence of the break-in.

Lee and Verna looked at each other as the same idea

occurred to both of them.

"Now's the time to pay another visit to the realtor."

"Now's the time to pray for God's will to be shown to us."

Monday morning found Lee and Verna at the real estate office.

"No," said the agent slowly, "the sellers have not changed their minds."

"In other words, the property is still for sale to anyone but us," Lee summed up.

"Sounds like it, doesn't it?" admitted the agent. "I dislike being a party to anything that even hints of discrimination."

"Do you know what is happening to the property?" asked Verna.

"What do you mean?"

"Just this: vandals have recently broken windows and gotten into the house. The interior has been damaged. We talked to the policeman who was investigating the vandalism."

"Not only that," added Lee, "but day by day the place looks increasingly deserted, neglected, and run-down. Shrubs and flowers are dying of neglect. Weeds are rampant. One break-in can lead to another, and the property will steadily decrease in value."

"As much as we want the property, we don't want to purchase a home half destroyed by vandalism," Verna concluded. "These people are only hurting themselves by stalling."

"This might be a persuasive point," the realtor said with a grin. "I'd like to get this one settled as much as you would. I'll call you back in a couple of days."

The longest two days Lee and Verna had known crawled by.

The call came on the third day. Verna was at the

phone instantly. The realtor's voice sounded cheerful. "I believe everyone in the family is going to sign this time," he said.

As he continued his description of the negotiations, Verna hardly heard him, for she was holding a little praise service for the Lord in her heart! Oh, thank You, Lord, for feeling You can trust us with this project!

What was that the realtor was saying?

"You know, it's funny that in all the time this property was on the market nobody came in even to inquire about it. On a main road, too. It wasn't exactly invisible, but it might as well have been."

"Praise the Lord," said Verna.

In a short time the final papers were signed.

One day not long after, Lee and Verna and their pastor went to the Indian Agency to discuss the proposed gift of an acre and a half of the land to the Upper Columbia Conference. As the land was already divided into the four tax lots, they simply combined two of the lots, and the agency gave its approval. The Clays' bank made arrangements to clear the land financially, and the conference accepted the donation.

The dream was coming closer to reality.

THE WAKE

AFTER HIS FATHER died, 16-year-old Billy felt totally displaced, belonging nowhere. His father, with whom he had lived for many years, had allowed him to do as he pleased. In his mother's home he felt completely alienated as she protested his being so rude and wild-acting. Billy had heard from his father that she was a bad woman, so he paid little attention to her. She loved him, but he was out of her control and in complete confusion as to how he fit in. With his father dead, he was no longer happy anywhere.

One night as friends brought him home from a party, he grew morose and silent. Depression settled upon him because there seemed to be no reason for him to go on living.

Getting out of the car at his mother's house, he stood in the dark as his friends drove away. A blackness settled about him. The urge to destroy himself became overpowering. As he turned toward the house, half a dozen lean, mangy dogs leaped, yelping, to greet him, but he struck at them blindly, and they slunk away.

The lights were out; no one was home. Well, I might as well end it all, he thought desperately as he switched on a light and searched for the loaded gun, kept high in a cupboard.

A sharp shot rang out in the still night, there was a thud, then silence.

Late the next morning Billy's mother, who had been staying with a sick relative, came home to find the door ajar and her young son lying dead in a pool of congealed blood. The gun lay on the floor where it had fallen. One of the dogs howled low and mournfully.

With a moan the stricken woman sank to her knees. Rocking back and forth, she began the wailing death chant that sent shivers through the chill morning air.

Later in the day Verna Clay found out about the suicide, and the next day, Friday, she took two dishes of food to Billy's mother as a token of concern. Billy's sister was at home. She explained that her mother was at the mortuary. Indian dead are never left alone; a relative is always present.

The daughter asked Verna to come to the services, which would begin that night at the long house. Verna, still weak from surgery, was unable to go that night, but on Sabbath afternoon, after Story Hour, the volunteer group went to the long house to pay their respects to the family.

Filing in rather self-consciously through the kitchen, where several women were preparing food, the group greeted the women and found their way into the long house. The casket was resting on a huge slab, with chairs and benches set up on two sides. Several drummers were beating out a rhythm that built up from near silence into a deafening cacophony of sound, then slowly diminished again into a whisper. Relatives sat around the casket. The head drummer had a place of honor by a table close to the casket. A bell was rung to accompany the drums, while a group of Indians sang a wailing chant. It was a very sad sound.

When the drums stopped, a man talked for a while in an Indian language.

The Story Hour group was seated in chairs around a table, then each of them was given a glass of water, such as each person in the room had. When the drums died down, everyone drank exactly one third of his water.

Finally, the drumming ended, and Billy's mother invited Verna and her group to stay for the meal. A great variety of food was served, including several types of native wild roots, which the visitors found interesting and appetizing.

After the meal Verna and Billy's mother visited together. The mother said, "I have always sympathized with other mothers who lost sons, but I didn't know how hard it was."

On Sunday morning Verna took to the long house a fruit plate for breakfast, and several loaves of bread for lunch, along with a great bunch of flowers. The wake still continued, with people coming and going, the drums throbbing, and intermittent speech-making.

Lee and Pastor Perry went back to the long house Sunday evening. The drumming was still going on. The men—relatives and friends of the deceased—dressed in their buckskin clothing, beads, and feathers, were hopping solemnly sideways around the casket in time with the rhythm of the drums. Later, young girls, also costumed beautifully, danced for a time about the casket.

The purpose of the whole ceremony, which lasted several days, was to petition the Great Spirit to accept the spirit of the deceased. Several times while Lee and the pastor were there, a speaker announced that if anyone wished to say something he could do so. Pastor Perry missed the cue. Later he found out that he could have conducted a complete Christian funeral service right then and there, during the wake, and was, in fact, expected to do so, but he did not know the custom. Later he learned that the more services held during a wake, the more the deceased is honored. But nobody explained the custom until later.

The final funeral service and burial was held on Monday.

"Well, we're learning the customs little by little, the hard way," the volunteers agreed after it was all over.

THE ROOT FESTIVAL

WITH THE PURCHASE of the reservation property completed, the Clays faced another problem. Their property in Stateline, which included a house, the shop, and a rental unit near the shop, remained on the market without selling.

"Amazing, since it is in an excellent location," puzzled the realtor. "But no one appears willing to buy that many lots, or to pay the price, or something."

Meanwhile Verna and Lee had to pay for the upkeep of both places on limited means. Verna was not at all well; small abscesses continued to form in her throat. But in spite of all the negatives, they determined to move to the new location on simple faith.

After they moved to the reservation, Verna tried working at a little electronics industry nearby, but the work was too hard and the tobacco smoke irritated her throat. She had to quit after a few weeks.

The Clays continued to look for ways to earn extra money. In sorting belongings for the move they found numerous items that they did not need so one day in late spring they announced a yard sale. It was Root Festival time on the reservation and many Indians had returned to celebrate.

Edible roots have been a diet staple of the Umatilla Indians for hundreds of years. And even though the gathering of roots is now restricted to small areas, the women are able to accumulate a quantity for the festival and some to dry for occasions later in the year.

During the yard sale Verna and Lee met a number of Indians whom they had not seen before. Lee talked with one woman who explained that she had come from the West Coast to see her relatives again and to celebrate the Root Festival.

"This is my childhood home. I am a member of the Wallawalla tribe," she said.

"I have heard something of the Root Festival, but I don't understand its significance. What does it mean to your group?" inquired Lee.

"Well, in the spring when the roots are at the peak of their growth," the woman began, "the Indian women go to the uncultivated lands in the hills and mountains to spend many days gathering, cleaning, processing, and drying the numerous different kinds of roots. Among these are the cous, or cowish, also known as biscuit root, which is one of the commonest edible roots. It can be eaten raw, boiled, mashed, or pressed into cakes and dehydrated for storage. There are flavorful wild onions of several kinds, wild carrots, bitterroot, and, of course, the western camass, which is delicious and sweet, either cooked or raw. We also use the roots of wild hyacinth, the seeds of the pond lily, the bulbs of the sego lily and the tubers of the arrowhead, or wapato.

"Many years ago our people harvested great quantities of these roots to store for winter in woven baskets, to go along with the dried salmon, dried wild game, and dried wild berries. My people raised no food crops; they lived from the abundance of the land, gathering only what they needed.

"Each year, after our women have gathered quantities of roots and the men have caught many salmon, we have a feast of celebration, during which we thank the Creator for providing us with food. We prepare the roots in many traditional ways and invite white people to eat with us and sample the roots with which they are not usually familiar.

"We believe that as long as we are thankful and celebrate this feast, the Creator will continue to provide us with food. With the coming of the white man, and subsequent cultivation, our gathering grounds have mostly disappeared, but in the higher hills some plants are still abundant.

"Even so, the earth is becoming more and more polluted. The time may come when we will no longer have our native wild foods.

"The earth is not the same as it was when it came from the hands of the Creator. But someday my people believe there will be a day of purification. Our legends have told of these things for thousands of years. It is our belief that when the Creator purifies the earth, He will then have a people on the earth who will obey Him."

"That is a most interesting story," exclaimed Lee. "Do you have a church affiliation?"

"Yes," she replied, "I belong to the American Indian religion."

"You seem to have some beliefs similar to ours. We believe, too, that the earth will be made new and God's people will someday dwell forever safely and peacefully. Here's a paper for you, so that you may know what we believe."

Later, Lee and Verna went to the Root Festival and

sampled some of the interesting foods with out-of-the-ordinary tastes. Their Indian friends urged them to try this and that dish, watching eagerly to see how they enjoyed it.

"How little we know of wild edibles, Lee," Verna mused. "We should have these folk show us how to find, dig, and prepare some of these good things."

"That could be another 'exchange item' along with native handicrafts," agreed Lee. "Just wait until we have a building of our own."

DOLLARS AND DONATIONS

WHILE VERNA and Lee Clay had been waiting for the reservation property to clear for sale, the Blue Mountain church members had considered ways and means to build the Indian center.

A number of negative factors were present. No money was available to buy anything. The local conference had as yet developed no policies regarding Indian work, nor had the union or General Conference formulated guidelines. An on-reservation mission was an unprecedented proposition, with questionable merit from the viewpoint of conference officials having to balance a restricted budget. Few if any conferences had made attempts at starting any type of statistically unrewarding specialized endeavors for ethnic groups living within the United States.

All along a few members said, "Just wait! You'll get the property, but you'll never obtain funds from the conference."

But Pastor Perry countered, "I think you're wrong. The timing seems to be right. I detect an interest on the conference level. If we can get the land and the donation worked out between the Clays, the Tribal Council, and the Upper Columbia Conference, we might come up with a little money."

Accordingly, even before the property was bought, Pastor Perry talked about the possibility of funding with local and union conference personnel. Among those he contacted was Elder Roger A. Wilcox, General Conference director of the missions program for North America. Elder Wilcox came to the area to discuss the proposed site and the tentative planning. He encouraged Pastor Perry and the Blue Mountain church to go right ahead with the plan. M. C. Torkelsen, the North Pacific Union Conference president, and Upper Columbia's president, Richard Fearing, also encouraged the church.

As soon as the Clays had purchased and donated the land, Pastor Perry applied to the local and union conferences for funding. Elder Torkelsen became so interested in the project that he thought up a variety of fund-raising strategies. He also came up with an "insta-church" plan that might work as a basic design for an Indian educational center. This was a fairly simple bolt-together building with a main floor that was normally movable. He, Pastor Perry, and his brother-in-law, Dick Lane, revised the plan for local need.

When the plan was taken to the local conference committee it decided to donate some money on condition that the union and the General Conference would match the funds.

The union conference had funds for new work and decided that the proposed Indian center fell into the right category. The General Conference also voted to appropriate funds.

But those appropriations were not sufficient. Inflation and the high cost of materials forced Pastor Perry to seek more funds. The union office gave money from inner city funds. Still he did not have enough. Back to the Upper Columbia Conference he went, to consult with Elder Torkelsen, who said, "I think I know where we can get a little more."

Application was made to a special Harris Pine Mills trust fund set aside for special projects such as this. Fund trustees agreed to donate $5,000 in 1979 and a similar amount in early 1980 for this local mission project, which would be situated only six miles away from the mills.

Eventually Pastor Perry raised $40,000, which was not very much money to construct a representative Indian center. Actually it was not even enough to buy basic building materials, let alone pay for labor, fees, and permits. But if this was the Lord's work, He would show the way.

Elder Torkelsen suggested asking for assistance from Maranatha Flights International, an Adventist volunteer organization composed of people who spend much of their spare time and means building projects all over the world that develop or improve educational, medical, or church facilities in needy areas. He referred Pastor Perry to local chapter president Larry Goodhew, a longtime member of MFI.

The more Larry listened to the pastor's outline of the proposed project, the more enthusiastic he became. This, he felt sure, would be an appropriate project for Maranatha.

He explained to the pastor that everything would need to be ready for the group to go to work as soon as they arrived. This meant that the foundation would have to be completed so that work could begin immediately on the superstructure, and all necessary materials would have to be on hand. The MFI members would look after their own transportation, but the local group would be responsible for room and board.

"We will set a tentative date for the volunteers to come," Larry said, "and I will contact members who might be available at that time."

"Fair enough," said Pastor Perry, who had been listening intently and throwing in a few questions from time to time.

Larry, who had just returned from a Maranatha project at Omak, Washington, apologized, "My wife, Jacquie, and I are scheduled for a church building project in the Azores, so I will be unable to coordinate this job at Mission. Why don't you contact my wife's cousin, John Kivett, of College Place, Washington? He is an experienced building contractor and would be just the man to direct the laying of the foundation and coordinate the Maranatha group project. Johnnie will also know all about obtaining building permits, as well as the best supply sources for possible at-cost purchasing. His guidance could cut the cost of building considerably. He would also know how to direct the volunteers so they can do the job most efficiently. That's how we can go into an area and complete a job in about two weeks."

"This sounds like the answer to our shoestring budget," said Pastor Perry. "You set the date and we'll be ready."

The pastor went home to plan how to make his request to Johnnie Kivett. Asking around locally about Johnnie, he heard some good reports.

"Oh, yes! You'd be lucky to get him. He's been contracting around here for about 30 years, and anything he builds is built well."

Armed with all this encouragement, a partially revised blueprint, and a wholly inadequate budget, Darrell Perry found the Birch Street address and knocked on the Kivett door.

FROM DREAM TO REALITY

STANDING AT THE Kivett door, Darrell Perry heard the sound of quick footsteps; then the door was flung open in response to his ringing the doorbell, by a slim, curly-haired man with a wide smile.

"Yes, sir!" the man exclaimed. "What can I do for you?"

"I'm Darrell Perry, pastor of the Blue Mountain church. For the past three and a half years some of my members have been holding a Story Hour for Indian children, over at Mission. Now these families are ready to build an Indian center on donated land. I've come to see you about coordinating the building project at Mission. Larry Goodhew directed me to you."

"I'm glad to meet you. We've just returned from Yakima. Larry told me a little about your plans the other day. Come in and let's talk about them."

Johnnie Kivett ushered Pastor Perry into the living room. The pastor settled his large frame comfortably on a sofa and unrolled his blueprints and specifications, as Johnnie's wife, Freddie, came in to be introduced.

He handed Johnnie a blueprint and explained what they had in mind.

"The basic floor plan is about all we will follow. We must have a full daylight basement to include a large craft and recreation room as well as smaller rooms for craft storage and giveaway items—you know, racks of clothing, and shelves for bedding and household items. There is room upstairs for only chapel, restrooms, and classrooms."

Johnnie studied the plans carefully. After a while he looked up and smiled. "These are workable plans, except for a few minor adjustments to conform to codes."

"On $40,000?"

"Not unless we can obtain most or all of the labor and materials at cost. We must include the permit, inspection, and hookup fees, labor for excavating the basement, constructing forms, and pouring cement. Let's get organized on preliminaries and see if we can save some time, too. Do you have a date for Maranatha yet?"

"I have a tentative date of October 21. Larry Goodhew will confirm it as soon as he hears from the volunteers he has contacted."

"About six weeks away. There's a lot to accomplish before we're ready for Maranatha volunteers to arrive. We'll both be busy."

"If I hadn't already seen and felt God's hand in this project," said Pastor Perry, "I'd say the whole thing is impossible."

"I know what you mean," Johnnie responded, "but I have just come back from my first two Maranatha projects, where I saw so many of God's providences that I'm reeling. The Lord is in this work, no question about it. Nothing is impossible with Him. And the more time we save by good planning and the use of existing funds, the more He will bless this job."

"I'm glad to hear you say that."

"I have a reason. As you know, I'm a builder. I have several acres here in College Place to subdivide and develop immediately. Until a few days ago my credit was good for a building loan up to half a million dollars anywhere in this valley. But now interest rates have shot up, building loans have become impossible to obtain, and today I can't borrow enough money to build a henhouse. My subdivision will have to wait until I once again can afford to borrow. So I just happen to have the time. I'll be glad to coordinate this job for you. While you see to the preliminary permits, let me find out how much I can save you on materials. I've done business with nearly all the local building suppliers."

After scrutinizing the plans thoroughly, the two men agreed that if they could get the basement done and an upstairs set upon it, they'd be stretching the $40,000 for all it was worth.

"But it's a start. It's the Lord's work, and whatever we need will come," Pastor Perry observed optimistically. "Our group has a meeting scheduled for a few nights from now at the Stateline church. I'd like for you to meet the people involved and put this plan before them. Please come if you can."

"I surely will," answered Johnnie. "There's a lot of planning to be done, and I'm sure we need input from the families who will be using the building."

A few days later the reservation tribal committee issued a zoning permit, as they had promised the Clays, and verbally approved sewer hookup to the Pendleton system. Next came a building permit. Pastor Perry gave the local State office a copy of the blueprint, telling the girl who received it to specify "unfinished basement."

Meanwhile Johnnie began soliciting some of the local building supply companies about discounts on material.

Most were congenial. One firm in Walla Walla agreed to sell building materials at cost price.

At the appointed time Johnnie met with the Clays, the Cripes, Dick and Hazel Lane, Pastor Perry and wife, and several other volunteers, who were enthusiastic over the plans and figures Johnnie presented.

Dick Lane volunteered to bring his new small tractor over to help.

"I didn't need the tractor," he admitted, "I just bought it on an impulse."

"Pretty good timing," complimented Johnnie.

"Yes, I know now why I bought it. This will be great for light work during construction," Dick grinned, his dark eyes sparkling. "As you know, I have had a particular interest in this mission ever since we moved here several months ago. My wife and Pastor Perry's wife are sisters, so we were introduced to the Story Hour project almost immediately. We've been helping as often as possible. These are my people. As I'm a Yakima Indian, I think I can help here in more ways than one. I'm disabled and on a pension, but I plan to be here every day that the Lord gives me strength."

"I've been told you're a carpenter, so I'm really glad you'll be on the job," agreed Johnnie. "Your tractor will come in handy many times during the building project. I can see where you'd fit well into the mission program, too. These Indian kids will respect you for what you are, not only as a Christian but as one of them."

"I just wish my tractor were large enough to dig that basement," Dick stated. "What are we going to do about that?"

"Well," said Pastor Perry, "we haven't found anyone to do it for free yet."

"I could trade an electrical job to pay for the use of a tractor," volunteered Ken Cripe.

"That might work," said Johnnie. "I have a backhoe, which I'll bring later. But we'll need a big blade for the initial excavating. I'll talk to my brother who lives in Pendleton to see if he knows of anyone who could help out."

Groundbreaking was scheduled for mid-afternoon on a September day. Early in the morning various members of the local team came in their camp trailers or motor homes. Others brought their camping equipment in during the day.

While the women set up housekeeping under the trees, the men looked over the site, which was all ready for excavation, and examined the big front loader tractor that had been brought in to do the excavating. Johnnie had found a man who volunteered to do the work for nothing.

"That big cat makes my Mitzi look like a miniature," Dick said with a laugh, looking fondly at his little tractor standing off to one side.

"But Mitzi can do things the big one can't, and we'll need her a good many times later," Johnnie assured him.

A big pickup drove in, kicking up a cloud of dust.

"Hi, Del!" yelled Johnnie as the driver emerged. "Come on over and meet these people."

Delwyn Nelson ambled over to shake hands all round.

"Del's going to do our initial excavating for us free of charge. As soon as I told him about the Mission project, he volunteered his time and his tractor until the job's done," explained Johnnie. "I don't think you can beat that."

"Shouldn't take long," Del smiled modestly. "I'm glad to help out on this kind of project. I don't belong to your church, but I think it's great what you're doing out here. Well, let's see what we'll need to do first."

"For free?" one of the group exclaimed. "You know

how much that'd cost if we had to pay for it?"

"We know," answered Dick.

"The Lord not only supplies our needs, He's generous," Johnnie confirmed, turning to follow Del, who was looking at the excavation site.

By three o'clock fifty-five persons had assembled for groundbreaking ceremonies. During the ceremony Elder J. D. Bolejack, associate director of Ministerial affairs for the Upper Columbia Conference, commended the Story Hour group for their courageous determination to construct an outreach center for the people of the Umatilla.

Within minutes after the ceremonies ended and guests had begun to leave, Lee and Verna stood hand in hand, watching the big tractor pushing earth and rock in front of the blade. As the dust rose and swirled in the afternoon breeze, Lee said, "I feel like I'm in a dream."

Verna sneezed. "I think the dust is real."

DAYS OF PREPARATION

DEL COMPLETED excavating within two days. Afterward Dick used his small tractor to level and square the excavation. He was proud of the way the sturdy little machine performed.

A volunteer plumber who came from the Blue Mountain church to do the plumbing had difficulty finding several key items. When he had just about decided he'd have to order them and possibly wait a long time for them, another plumber in Pendleton went to a job he was working on, took the needed parts, which he had already installed, and donated them so that installation could proceed on schedule. The layout was inspected and approved, subject to hookup, without any delay.

Late in the afternoon, three days later, Johnnie looked over at Dick, who was busily pegging a final form, and said, "Dick, isn't it surprising that in all this solid river rock the pegs are going in without breaking?"

Dick stood up slowly and replied solemnly, "The only thing that has broken today is my back. But we'll be ready to pour footings tomorrow. These have really gone in fast, like putting toothpicks into cheese."

Johnnie laughed. "You know, Dick, we'll have to do something about portable outhouses before long. We're OK now, but more people will be coming to help in just a few days and we'll need sanitary facilities. Do you know any place around Pendleton where we could rent a couple?"

"No, I don't." Dick tilted his head as he heard a pickup door slam. "Who's that?"

"Hi, fellas!" interrupted a voice from the bank above. "Look what I've brought you!"

Johnnie quickly clambered out of the basement. There in the back of a truck was a nice white portable toilet, the kind used on construction sites.

"Why, Johnnie," the newcomer exclaimed, "I didn't know you were on this job! Now I know why I felt such a strong impression to come out this way. Tell me, where do you want this little gem?"

Nearly speechless with surprise, Johnnie indicated the right spot and helped his friend unload the unit.

Curious, Dick asked, "How did you know we needed one of these?"

"I didn't. I was actually transporting it back to the shop in Walla Walla from the Roundup grounds when I had the strongest urge to drive out this way. No reason for it, because this is several miles out of my way. But I followed the impulse, noticed that you didn't have any sanitary facilities yet, and just sorta came on in."

"Well, what d'ya know!" exclaimed Dick wonderingly.

"Johnnie, is this your job?" asked the man.

"No," answered Johnnie, "although I'm coordinating it. Dick, tell him what this is all about."

So Dick explained about the volunteer project to build a Christian center for his fellow Indians and that many persons would be donating their labor, including a group called Maranatha Flights International, who would be coming in just a month to raise the walls and put on the roof.

The man listened, fascinated.

"Funny thing about it," Dick added, "we were talking about the need for sanitary facilities just when you were driving in."

"That is why we were so speechless," Johnnie added laughingly.

"So you're going to have thirty or forty more workers for a couple of weeks?"

"Yes, at least that many and sometimes more, when local volunteers show up. We will also have a group of college students for a day, and a class of high school students here to donate a day's work just before Maranatha arrives."

"You're going to need two of these!" the man exclaimed.

"That's about right," answered Johnnie.

"Tell you what I'll do. I have another unit coming off another project in about three weeks, and I'll just bring it right over here. It'll be set up by the time the crowd arrives."

"Man, we sure appreciate this. How much do we owe you?" asked Dick.

"Nothing at all," he replied. "You see, I owe Johnnie a favor. One time I was in a tight spot on a building project, and he pulled himself off a job he was on to help me. So this'll be my chance to return a very big favor. So long. I'll see you in a few weeks."

Dick stared after the departing truck. "Well, what d'ya know!"

"Seems like I've heard you say that once before, today," Johnnie observed. "The Lord has done it again.

His miracles cover every need!"

The workday was just about over when Ken Cripe drove in from his job and waved as he went to his mobile home nearby.

"You know, that's really something, the way Ken and Juanita sold everything they owned in Pendleton and moved out here to live on the reservation, isn't it?" said Johnnie.

"Yes," answered Dick, "Ken said he and Juanita wanted to be a part of this, so as soon as the Clays bought the property they rented the back lot, and out they came."

"Quite a garden they have coming on."

"They're hoping it will help feed the Maranatha group."

"Juanita's a good cook. I enjoy eating dinner there."

"She says we'll work better if we're well fed," said Dick. "I just hope she doesn't work too hard. Her health isn't very good. My wife is going to help her as soon as more people start coming."

Almost every day Johnnie brought another truckload of lumber and other materials to stockpile for Maranatha. By the last week in September the basement forms were nearing completion. Toward the end of the week Dick Lane asked, "Aren't we nearly ready for inspection? I suppose it will take the man quite a while to get here?"

"Yes on both," said Johnnie, glancing up from his work. "We'd better call the inspector today."

"I'll give him a ring next time I go to the house," Ken Cripe, who was working with them, offered.

But Ken never made the call, for within five minutes the inspector wheeled into the parking area and strode over to where the men were working.

"Hi, fellas," he called. "You about ready for me?"

Johnnie's eyes registered astonishment, but he

grinned matter-of-factly. "We sure are," he answered.

After the inspector walked about for a few minutes, he returned to Johnnie, saying, "Looks good! Go ahead and pour cement. Here's the approval."

"Thanks, sir." Johnnie accepted the paper. "You saved us at least a day by coming when you did. Now we'll be able to start pouring the first of the week. Thanks again!"

As the inspector drove away, Dick, who had been watching in wonderment, broke the silence.

"Well——" he began.

Johnnie glanced at him quickly, and joined in, "What d'ya know!" They finished together, laughing.

Ken raised an eyebrow and said quietly, " 'Before they call, I will answer.' "

"Literally," said Johnnie.

A few days later, after the cement was poured, Pastor Perry applied for permission to hook up the plumbing. But the city of Pendleton would not allow hookup without a letter from the Umatilla Tribal Council. City officials appeared doubtful that the council would give approval. As Pastor Perry turned to leave he said, "I'll be right back."

The official shook his head and replied, "I doubt that very much."

When Pastor Perry appeared at the tribal office to ask for the letter, the man looked surprised. "But we gave verbal approval."

Pastor Perry smiled. "I know you did, but you know how city officials are. They want something in writing to put into their files."

The man turned to a coworker. "Do I have the authority to write this letter?" he asked.

"Yes, as far as I know."

In a few minutes Pastor Perry had a typed letter to

take back to the Pendleton office. When he walked in that same afternoon, a few jaws dropped with surprise. City officials had been certain that the tribal council would not even approve, to say nothing of furnishing that approval in writing.

After considerable debate the officials decided to count this as a private dwelling and to charge on that basis, which was much less than for a public building.

"Another day, another penny saved," sang Pastor Perry as he headed back toward the building site with the good news.

The plumber found that he needed a special saddle to fit into the street hookup. He and Pastor Perry searched through plumbing shops all over the valley trying to find one. Finally, a clerk in one shop accidentally found the needed part in the bottom of a box. That solved the hookup problem.

Next, the basement floor needed to be readied for pouring. Early in October a group of Walla Walla Valley Academy students and teachers donated the equivalent of 25 working days helping to prepare the floor for pouring and painting the prefab walls with primer. With their help nearly everything was primed before bad weather arrived.

Then, a week later, 26 Walla Walla College students and teachers from the Industrial Technology Club came to work on the basement and put in the floor joists. They also put down the subflooring. Verna Clay had 38 persons for dinner that day.

The men decided that good wooden shingles, or shakes, would be better than composition shingles, and found an excellent bargain in Weippe, Idaho.

Dick Lane and Johnnie drove to Weippe for a load of shakes around the middle of October. By that time the weather was becoming cold, and the roads were sometimes hazardous. As they were driving back, their heavily-loaded truck suddenly slid around end for end on an icy hill. But it stayed on the road and they were able to head it in the right direction once more and continue, somewhat shaken, on their way, thanking the Lord for His care. Later Dick and another volunteer trucked a second load of shakes. So close was their estimate that there were only a half-dozen shakes left over when the roof was finished.

With the foundation and other preliminaries completed, building materials stockpiled and ready, and camper space cleared, Johnnie and his crew felt ready for Maranatha Flights International. Next door, at the Clays, volunteer cooks had been busy for several weeks feeding resident and visiting volunteers and stockpiling quantities of food for the anticipated MFI crowd. Pastor Perry had asked Dick Lane's wife, Hazel, to be in charge of food preparation for the main group. Now all was ready for the Maranatha crowd. The evening before the Maranatha group was to arrive, clouds rolled in thick and heavy, and rain began to fall. Johnnie and his wife, Freddie, who had driven over for the weekend, gazed at each other and moaned, "Oh, no!"

MARANATHA MIRACLES

ALL NIGHT LONG the rain fell. At times it slackened off briefly, and hopes rose within the campers. Then it started afresh, and despair began to set in throughout the ranks. Listening to the drumming of drops on the camper roof, Johnnie remarked to Freddie, "With 40 or 50 volunteers coming to raise the walls tomorrow, the weather had better break!"

Everyone was up for the 6:30 breakfast, and the warm food somehow made the chilly, wet dawn seem brighter. Several Maranatha workers had come in a day early, so there was quite a crowd for the meal.

The group agreed to do what could be done, in spite of the rain. "Unless we get to work," Johnnie declared thoughtfully, "we can't ask the Lord to stop the rain."

"That's true," chorused several voices.

"And," boomed Pastor Perry, striding in with dripping jacket, "that's what we're going to do right now. Let's ask God to stop the rain and then get right out there and show Him we mean business!"

"Amen," everybody exclaimed.

But the sun didn't come out until the volunteers began to work at their assigned tasks.

Throughout the morning, campers, motor homes, and trailers poured into the camping area. In addition to Maranatha members, volunteers from local churches came for the day.

Local residents driving by that day had a lot to observe. Many slowed down or stopped to watch the line of 48 workers raising a 72-foot section of wall into place. As soon as that was fastened, the other walls went up. And suddenly a building was taking shape.

That night the wind began to blow. Pendleton winds can be violently gusty and destructive. More than one worker slipped out of bed to venture out into the wet, windy night to see if the walls were holding.

Next morning everyone was thankful to see them still standing sturdily. Eventually the weather cleared up, making for more pleasant working conditions.

One day Johnnie's backhoe quit functioning when a hydraulic line broke. He had been using it to lift shakes to the roof of the building. He knew repairs could be costly, but Pastor Perry contacted LaVerne Nelson, a mechanic who was a member of the Blue Mountain church, to see if he could help. The replacement part cost $18; Mr. Nelson donated his time to install it. After that there was no more trouble with the backhoe.

A sheriff's deputy, who stopped by to see the work, asked Verna Clay what was happening. When she told him about Maranatha volunteers and the purpose for the Indian center, he said, "If you save even one person, it's worth the effort."

MARANATHA WINE

A HAPPY, NOISY group of workers assembled for each evening meal at Verna's house. She had set up tables in the living and family rooms to accommodate them all.

"Just look at all that food, folks," said one, looking at the piles of donated fruit and vegetables.

Hazel Lane and her volunteers were just plain thankful for the food. Some of the produce was from Ken and Juanita's garden. Ken had started a garden at the back of the Clay property in the spring of 1979, and it grew bigger and bigger as he brought home seeds and more seeds to plant.

"Why are we planting this big garden?" Juanita asked.

"There must be a reason," Ken answered cheerfully.

"What'll we do with all of it?"

"Oh, it won't go to waste."

Now Ken smiled as he brought in a big box of newly-picked sweet corn for dinner. He had not only enough for his own needs, but plenty for everyone else. It had matured in time to feed the four volunteers who worked on the project before Maranatha, and now that the MFI volunteers were there, he had more than enough to feed them. In addition, he had ripe tomatoes, peppers, cabbage, sprouts, beets, carrots, all sorts of root vegetables, greens, and salad makings in abundance.

"Now we know why we planted so much garden," he told Juanita. "The Lord knew all along we'd need it."

Corn lasted until frost, and no one tired of it.

Several weeks before October 21, local church bulletins had announced the coming of Maranatha volunteers and the need for donations of food. From then on people began bringing food to Verna Clay's kitchen. Sometimes someone would knock at the back door as she was letting another person in at the front door. Hazel Lane, who was coordinating food service, worked with a volunteer to set up tables for vegetables, fruit, frozen foods, and hot dishes.

Food flowed through the house and out onto the back porch. Several packing houses donated boxes of fruit, such as apples and pears. Winter squash and sacks of potatoes piled up in corners. When Jim Wells came in with a supply of canned food he asked, "What else do you need, ladies?"

"Eggs!" they chorused.

He was soon back with eight dozen, which stayed fresh until used.

Ken Cripe's cousin, Ed, owned a vineyard but was no longer selling his grapes to a commercial cannery. He decided that he would donate or sell for Sabbath school Investment whatever ripened. That was all it took to guarantee a bumper crop. He had never raised such sweet grapes, hanging heavy on the vines. Ed brought Juanita eight boxes of prime, ripe grapes. Juanita wondered what to do with them. But the next day someone donated dozens of jars so volunteers canned gallons of grape juice. Ed came with batch after batch of grapes. Some of the grapes Juanita sold, and Ed donated the proceeds to Investment.

Strange about that grape crop! Other vineyards in the valley did poorly, while Ed's grapes grew large and abundant.

Proprietors of a nursing home in Pendleton donated many cans of orange juice. Doris Tucker brought in jars of grapefruit juice she had preserved months before while living in California. She told the cooks she hadn't known why she had canned so much, until now. She felt that was a sort of miracle too. No one could disagree.

Excess tomatoes, apples, and pears were canned as they came in, to keep them from spoiling and to have them when needed. The Clays preserved enough apples to put one in each of 100 sacks of goodies that the Story Hour group handed out to Indian children at a Christmas party in the long house in December.

Johnnie's wife, Freddie, brought quantities of donated food from College Place and Walla Walla on her weekend trips to Mission. Rolls, bread, cookies, casseroles, all came just when needed.

Pastor Perry, expecting a large expense for food, was amazed to see the amount of food donated, and pleased to see it continued to come in as needed during the two weeks of Maranatha participation.

One Thursday the cooks were wondering what to fix for the next day, when the doorbell rang unexpectedly. Hazel Lane came back bringing two large casseroles.

"Ladies," she announced, "here's part of tomorrow's dinner."

An Indian woman to whom Verna had given some sweet corn noticed the crowd of people eating at Verna's house and brought a large salmon. Although she didn't quite know what to do with it, Verna could not refuse, because the gift of a salmon from a Umatilla Indian is a special gesture. She quietly gave the salmon away, but the "moccasin phone" works wondrously well. The Indian woman became very upset at what she had done and told Verna bluntly that the Salmon was for her, and nobody else. So Verna's trial-and-error learning process continued.

On the final Sabbath of Maranatha, 81 people attended dinner at Verna's house. All volunteers insisted this was about the best food they'd had on any project. The next day, after the Maranatha volunteers had gone, the cooks stayed on to can and freeze the remaining food to use for the few workers who were still on the job.

During the two weeks the Maranatha volunteers were on the job they averaged 240 man hours a day, valued at thousands of dollars in terms of labor costs. No one was hurt; as Johnnie reported, the biggest injury was covered with a band aid. And everyone stayed happy and healthy on all the good food and fresh grape juice, which they called Maranatha wine.

Best of all, Pastor Perry stayed within his budget!

THE PHANTOM BASEMENT

BUT YOU DON'T even have a basement!" the Pendleton fire safety inspector protested.

"Oh, yes, we do; our upstairs is not resting on thin air," laughed Pastor Perry. "I gave you the information on the unfinished basement when I applied for the building permit."

The pastor had gone in to the office to ask about a number of items in connection with planning to finish the basement, now that the money designated to complete the downstairs would soon be forthcoming. Already the basement had studded walls, with plumbing and electricity completed.

The inspector continued to study the blueprint. He looked up, puzzled. "We have a problem."

"What information can I furnish you that may help?" asked Pastor Perry.

"Draw a rough schematic of the basement and we'll decide."

A few days later Pastor Perry presented the sketch to the building inspector, who called in a local deputy fire inspector and another building inspector. They all sat down together to decide whether it would be necessary to have a sprinkling system and a fire door that would hold up for three hours in case of fire. New state policies indicated that both would probably be necessary.

"What is your water source?" asked the inspector.

"A well," Pastor Perry answered.

The man paled visibly. "You can't hook a sprinkling system to a well!"

"We must find some other way around this," said the deputy inspector. "What building usage category is it in?"

"Well, the building occupancy group is 101," said Pastor Perry.

"That puts it into a different code. You say the area is over 1500 square feet?"

Pastor Perry nodded.

"Let's see what the code book says."

The three officials spent several minutes studying the code book. Finally the inspector said, in mock disgust, "You and your phantom basement!"

"At least you have an excuse for losing us." Pastor Perry laughed. "You moved your office and lost us somewhere in between."

"I'll never know how," said the inspector, "but your whole building program probably would have been delayed for several months had we not lost it."

"Then I'll consider it providential," said Pastor Perry.

"Now, if you don't want another considerable delay, from one to four months," the inspector advised, "you'd better take this problem straight to the State building inspector's office in Salem and put your request directly to the man in charge. If you submit it in writing to us it could be summer before you receive a decision."

"Thanks for your advice. We want to start on the basement as soon as we receive our funds in mid-February, so I'll do as you suggest."

After getting an appointment with the State building inspector, Pastor Perry drove out to Mission, where Dick Lane and Don Kimple worked daily on the new building in spite of the formidable early-January weather.

"Dick, how would you like to go to Salem with me to see the building inspector?"

"Sure thing, if I can help," said Dick cheerfully.

"We'll start early Monday morning. Bad weather is predicted, but I think we can make it."

"Couldn't be worse than the road to Milton," Don said wryly. "We've spun around on the ice several times coming here the past few mornings. But Dick would just turn around and point the Bronco in the right direction and come on."

On the way to Portland the two men listened to radio reports of freezing rain and dangerous roads but found only a few icy spots. From Portland the freeway to Salem was better.

When the building inspector's secretary went into his office to announce that Pastor Perry and Dick had arrived to meet their appointment, Pastor Perry over-heard him say, "Oh, yes, I know what their problem is."

"Oh-oh!" he whispered to Dick, "I wonder what that means!"

As they were ushered into the inspector's office, Pastor Perry said, "I really appreciate your secretary. She went beyond the call of duty and mailed me a map showing how to get here. That really helped."

Mr. Johnson looked pleased. "That's the way she is," he replied.

As the men presented their problem the congenial inspector listened carefully. He was most interested in the purpose of the building and asked many questions. He seemed to understand their budget limitations.

"I know what the problems are like on the reservations. I once worked on the Navajo Reservation," Mr. Johnson said with a smile.

Dick's reserve began to thaw a little. This man had knowledge of the needs of the Indians and was sympathetic.

"Let's subtract walls and stairways from the floorspace and see if we can come up with less than 1500 square feet," the inspector continued.

He and Dick soon had the footage worked out. Eliminating space taken by walls and stairwells, they came to an estimate of just two square feet under the limit.

"I think we can exempt you from needing a sprinkler system in the basement. And that should save you a lot of money."

"We checked the cost, and it's absolutely formidable. It could wipe us out financially," agreed Pastor Perry.

"I'll call the State fire marshal to make sure we're within legal limits."

The fire marshal agreed, deciding that they wouldn't even need a fire door at the end of the basement. The men thanked him for his help, then thanked Mr. Johnson for saving them so much time and money.

"Well, we can stay within our tight budget, after all," remarked Pastor Perry as he and Dick drove back toward the freeway.

"He was the right man to see."

"With his background of working with the Indians, he surely was," agreed Pastor Perry.

"This trip saved a lot of dollars, and we can now begin working on the basement that isn't supposed to be there," Dick observed.

By late March, 1980, the basement was finished sufficiently to use for Pathfinder meetings, classes, and other activities.

Dick and Hazel Lane, who headed the Pathfinder Club, had a lively group. The older children appeared to be enjoying the activities planned for them by the Lanes, which included a weekend trip to the mountains and a kite-flying contest, during which the youngsters flew kites they had made during Pathfinder crafts classes.

The Indians began to accept the new building and to call it "our building" among themselves.

JUST A BEGINNING

BECAUSE OF THE upsurge of interest in reaching the various ethnic groups living within the boundaries of North America, most of the union conferences are establishing a department of human relations, to study needs, methods of evangelizing, and policies in that area. A. Leroy Moore is coordinator of native American work in the North American Division.

Work among black and Spanish American segments of the population is progressing rapidly. In the North Pacific Union Conference, E. A. White currently heads the human relations committee, which is scheduled to meet twice a year to work out problems with minority groups and to make plans for minorities. Walla Walla College has established a special fund for helping any Indian who wishes to study there. These may be slow beginnings, but at least there is movement.

Interest in missions for native Americans became apparent when the Washington Conference laid plans, in December, 1979, for a more active ministry by church members among the Indians of the Pacific Northwest.

The Clays and Pastor Perry attended the meeting to represent the first permanently established Seventh-day Adventist mission in the Northwest on reservation land. Delegates expressed interest in starting similar mission projects on the Colville, Nez Percé and Yakima reservations. The need is great among the Warm Springs and Klamath tribes in Oregon. Montana members have expressed an interest in starting new work among the Indian populations in that State.

The delegates learned that 68,000 Indians live in the Pacific Northwest States, 70,000 more living in Alaska, with a total of 875,000 Indians in the United States. Canada has thousands more. So many need to be reached; there is an important work to do. The Indians of North America do not merely need another church. Their needs are greater than that. The mission is one endeavor to meet the greater need.

The mission's program is an ongoing one. In January, 1980, Dick and Hazel Lane began a Pathfinder Club. By February, 1981, membership had grown to about 40 children, who were participating in classes in which first aid, electricity, plaster art, embroidery, photography, and other things were being taught.

The Story Hour leaders are planning to revive native arts, as well as to teach such crafts as knitting, crocheting, quilting, sewing, cooking, child care, and nutrition. Smoking, alcohol, and weight-control clinics are in the planning stage also. Lee Clay wants to start classes in various trades, such as electricity and welding, for men.

On October 25, 1980, the Indian Adventist Center, completely finished inside and out and attractively landscaped, was dedicated free of debt. Members formed a small church company on the same day. A few Indians are beginning to come to the center for special programs.

But many long-held grievances remain in the hearts of the Indians to deter them from becoming interested in Christianity. As one of them told Lee Clay during a feast to which the Clays were invited, "The white man broke his promises and stole our land. So why should I want to know about the white man's God?"

This attitude must be changed. A tremendous challenge faces not only the members of the Umatilla Indian Adventist Center, but all of us who are responsible to introduce Jesus to the thousands of other native Americans on reservations in the United States and Canada.

"I heard the voice of the Lord, saying, Whom shall I send, and who shall go for us?" (Isa. 6:8).